Stephen A. Royle studied geography at St John's College, Cambridge and then took a PhD at the University of Leicester. He moved to Belfast in 1976 to a lectureship in geography at Queen's University, where he is now professor of island geography. His books include *North America: a geographical mosaic* (edited with Frederick W. Boal, 1999); *A geography of islands: small island insularity* (2001); *Enduring city: Belfast in the twentieth century* (edited with Frederick W. Boal, 2006); *The company's island: St Helena, company colonies and the colonial endeavour* (2007); *Doing development differently: regional development on the Atlantic periphery* (edited with Susan Hodgett and David Johnson, 2007) and *Company, crown and colony: the Hudson's Bay Company and territorial endeavour in western Canada* (2011). Stephen Royle is treasurer of the International Small Island Studies Association, deputy editor of *Island Studies Journal*, chair of the Northern Ireland region of the Royal Geographical Society and former president of the Ulster Society for Irish Historical Studies, the Geographical Society of Ireland and the Belfast branch of the Geographical Association. He is a Member of the Royal Irish Academy.

PORTRAIT OF AN INDUSTRIAL CITY

'Clanging Belfast', 1750–1914

STEPHEN A. ROYLE

THE BELFAST NATURAL HISTORY
AND PHILOSOPHICAL SOCIETY
IN ASSOCIATION WITH
ULSTER HISTORICAL FOUNDATION

THE BELFAST NATURAL HISTORY AND PHILOSOPHICAL SOCIETY, founded in 1821, encourages understanding of the human and natural environment of Ireland, both past and present. It has a particular focus on Belfast and its hinterland. It promotes original scholarship, and new ideas and interpretations, which are of an academic standard and yet are accessible to a wider audience.

First published 2011
by the Belfast Natural History and Philosophical Society
www.belfastsociety.com
in association with Ulster Historical Foundation
49 Malone Road, Belfast, BT9 6RY
www.booksireland.org.uk

Distributed by Ulster Historical Foundation

Front cover: HOYFM.HW.H1915
Hand-riveters at work near Britannic bow, 25 May 1913
© National Museums Northern Ireland
Collection Harland & Wolff, Ulster Folk & Transport Museum

Printed manufacture by Jellyfish Print Solutions
Design by Cheah Design

CONTENTS

LIST OF ILLUSTRATIONS

LIST OF TABLES

NOTES

The following abbreviations have been used in the notes:

BCM	Belfast Corporation minutes
BL	British Library
BNL	*Belfast News Letter*
LHL	Linen Hall Library
LMA	Linen Merchants' Association
PRONI	Public Record Office of Northern Ireland

PREFACE: 'CLANGING BELFAST'

> The docks and quays are busy with their craft and shipping, upon the beautiful borders of the Lough; the large red warehouses stretching along the shores, with ships loading, or unloading, or building, hammers *clanging*, pitch pots flaming and boiling ... [author's emphasis]
>
> William Makepeace Thackeray.[1]

A Belfast councillor, Dr Henry O'Neill, wrote at the start of the twentieth century on the 'progress of sanitary science', stating that 'there is not a city in Ireland (if indeed any in the United Kingdom) which has so rapidly developed itself from insignificance to vast importance as Belfast'.[2] This book will consider Belfast's journey from the mid-eighteenth century to the eve of the Great War. The first chapter deals with Belfast's growth. The engine driving the town (then city) along this path was industry and that topic forms the subject matter of Chapter 2. That the engine did not carry all groups and people to ease and prosperity will become clear, especially when political and social issues are discussed in Chapters 3 and 4 respectively.

Anybody writing about Belfast in the period covered here must acknowledge having benefited from the works of modern scholars, whose publications will be cited appropriately below. Many of these scholars are historians but this author is a geographer. Such a distinction may strike the reader as arcane, but maybe there is some truth in the old (and gendered) adage that history is about chaps and geography about maps. Perhaps a geographer does bring to the table a sense of place, an appreciation of the significance of location, a realisation that decisions, from where to locate a shipyard to where to run in a riot, are affected by spatial considerations. Certainly, an historian who has read the author's work reported on his 'different approach', which was attributed to his geographical leanings. Perhaps the subtitle, 'Clanging Belfast', is part of this – a reference to contemporary activity rather than contemporary discourse. The title was chosen to try to particularise Belfast in its industrial era, when (and where) the soundscape would have emanated from the factories and shipyards. Early engineering and manufacture was characterised by much noisy physicality, by machines and people manipulating resources to make finished products, be they delicate linen handkerchiefs or mighty ships. Thackeray captured some essence of this with his observation of the hammers clanging in the shipyards, from which comes the subtitle.

Where possible, primary documentation has been consulted as a source of information for this study. This has included the minute books of Belfast Corporation and a hitherto little-used source, the annual reports of the Linen Merchants' Association. Newspapers, particularly the *Belfast News Letter*, have been very useful. The author was in receipt of a Small Research Grant from the British Academy to assist in the primary research. The grant meant that Dr Edwin Aiken could be employed as research assistant; to him, and not for the first time in print, the author records his thanks.

In addition, the author has turned to contemporary commentators who left much of inestimable value, such as two clergymen who detailed the life and conditions of the poor in Belfast in the 1850s, William O'Hanlon and Anthony McIntyre. Drs Andrew Malcolm and Henry O'Neill wrote on health and sanitation, D.J. Owen on the port, William Topping on life in the linen mills. There is material from contemporary fiction or commentary to add insight; some of which has been accessed via Patricia Craig's collection, *The Belfast anthology*.[3] There are various parliamentary papers to wade through. The two fascicles of the *Irish historic towns atlas* on Belfast contain much data and detail. Another source was W.R. Rodgers's 1955 radio broadcast, *The return room*, really a long poem reminiscent of *Under Milk Wood*, which evoked his early century Belfast childhood. Its welcome publication by Blackstaff Press came in 2010.[4]

This book is illustrated principally in two ways. There are a number of reproductions from historic Ordnance Survey maps of Belfast, whilst Figure 1.6 was drawn especially for this work by Maura Pringle of the School of Geography, Archaeology and Palaeoecology at Queen's University Belfast, to whom thanks are due. With one exception, the other figures are photographs taken by the author in an attempt to get away from the almost over-familiar Victorian and Edwardian images – to emphasise that, despite its post-modern, post-industrial glass and steel manifestation, Belfast still reflects many aspects of that remarkable era of its development: the 'clanging city', the industrial settlement of the late eighteenth to early twentieth centuries.

NOTES

1 William Makepeace Thackeray, *The Irish sketchbook* (London, 1842), p. 353 (Collins ed.).
2 Henry O'Neill, 'The progress of sanitary science in Belfast' in *Journal of the Statistical and Social Inquiry Society of Ireland*, xi (1901), p. 36.
3 Patricia Craig (ed.), *The Belfast anthology* (Belfast, 1999).
4 W.R. Rodgers, *The return room* (Belfast, 2010) (broadcast by Northern Ireland Home Service, 23 December 1955).

1
'THE TOWN BROKE LOOSE': GROWTH

'Foul leprous dens' and 'new houses and streets of the best description': boundaries, housing and socio-spatial patterns in Belfast

'Under the control which the corporation can exercise': boundaries
Belfast's population grew from an estimated 8,549 in 1757 to 386,946 in 1911, the date of the last census before the partition of Ireland, and 415,151 in 1926, the date of the first census afterwards.[1] This was largely through migration; at the 1901 census only twenty per cent of the city's household heads had been born there.[2]

At first the newspapers would carry simple factual reports on Belfast's population total whenever census results came out, as in 1813 and 1821.[3] Later, they would express pride at the rate of expansion. In the second half of the eighteenth century, notices would often be placed advertising land being leased for building to accommodate the growing settlement. For example, in 1757 one edition advertised plots at Malone, the Short Strand (just a few perches from the Long Bridge), the Long Strand and 'two good pasture fields near the end of the Long Bridge and adjoining the new road to Newton [Newtownards Road] very convenient for houses and gardens to be made thereon'.[4] During that period a notice appeared that Belfast land was to be surveyed 'according to the best and newest methods',[5] although it was to be another eighty years before the Ordnance Survey would do that job so thoroughly. George Benn wrote in 1823:

> old inhabitants … look in vain for the haunts of their youth, and at last discover that the places which had peacefully submitted, in their early years, to the spade or ploughshare are now covered with streets and habitations.[6]

One such inhabitant confirmed this, writing in 1827 that 'the town broke loose beyond its ancient limits … engrossing all the town parks and neat gardens I remember'.[7] Other land became available as the small docks of the town's pre-industrial core were filled in, such as May's Dock in 1844.[8] It was announced in 1847 that Town Dock, Lime Kiln Dock and Ritchie's Docks would be reclaimed inside two years,[9] whilst 'Victoria Square, now spacious and airy, was used as a

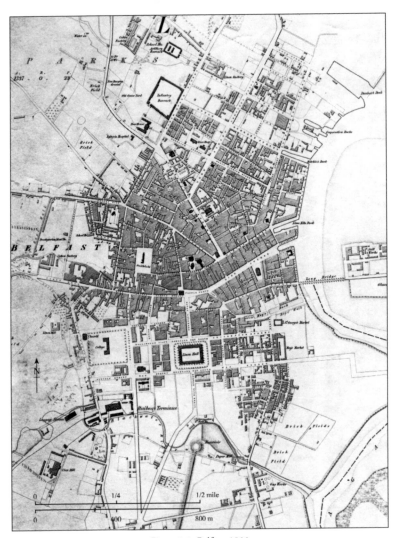

Figure 1.1 Belfast, 1833

timber pond'.[10] Such developments were just part of a more extensive
programme of land reclamation that transformed Belfast's waterfront
and provided room for port facilities and much of its industrial growth,
especially the shipyards. In similar fashion, the Farset River along High
Street, where the original docks were sited, was culverted, 'arching over
in a substantial manner', as an 1804 report had it. One benefit
identified was that accidental drownings would thus be expected to
decrease, for which the 'gentlemen of the Police Committee are
therefore entitled to the thanks of the community'.[11]

The pace of growth accelerated; at almost every meeting of the
council throughout the second half of the nineteenth century
permission was granted to build new streets and often other
infrastructural investments, including markets, lighting and sewers, as
well as for industrial development and public buildings. Acts of
parliament were required on occasion. For example, the Belfast
Improvement Act of 1845, amongst other matters, granted the council
powers to:

- widen existing streets;
- open new streets;
- regulate the width of future streets;
- provide and illuminate public clocks;
- secure yards and conveniences;
- provide public conveniences;
- enclose open grounds;
- enclose dangerous places;
- provide a pound;
- provide new markets;
- provide weighing machines and measuring houses;
- provide public slaughterhouses;
- construct common sewers;
- suppress gambling and cock-fighting and houses and
    places of improper resort.[12]

The boundaries of the town had to be adjusted to incorporate this
growth, as in 1836. In the proposal for the next extension, an 1853
report by Captain Francis Yarde Gilbert of the Royal Engineers,
comments about Belfast's industrial development, particularly in linen,

appeared; it was also noted that the port had grown to become the largest in Ireland. There had been associated population growth. Gilbert remarked that the Boundary Commissioners had estimated Belfast's population at 68,383 in 1836, but he now calculated it to be 115,294, including some 18,000 who lived outside the earlier boundary – hence the need for the extension. Reporting on his public consultations on the proposals, Gilbert commented that some people opposed any boundary extension just because it would place them 'under the control which the corporation can exercise as to supervision and taxation'. An appendix to his report listed sixty-two signatories to one such letter of protest.[13] Nevertheless, most proprietors and mill owners accepted the need for an extension for the general good, for as things stood:

> From the number of hands employed in the manufactories and the necessity of their having houses contiguous for residence, buildings are erected in every direction and from want of supervision of a responsible body the streets are deficient in order, paving and sanitary condition. Houses for mechanics in a growing industrial town, built according to the mere object or interest of the owner or builder, or the exigency of the occasion, require constant and stringent control, and on my inspection of the suburbs beyond the present boundary, I found generally in those lately erected, the streets narrow, irregular, unpaved and in many places impassable, no regular system of sewerage, a deficiency of yards and other accommodation and courts narrow and confined, built inside streets.[14]

Gilbert noted that Belfast was growing strongly to the west; there were considerable rafts of low-quality housing extending up the Falls and Shankill Roads especially that did lie beyond the old borough boundary. However, his observations perhaps failed to acknowledge the considerable amount of poor-quality housing existing at this period inside the old boundary (which will be discussed below), although he did comment that the council had 'purchased and pulled down several streets in the old and decayed part of the town and erected new and wide streets in their places'.[15]

The council pressed for another extension in 1896.[16] This came about through the operation of the Belfast Corporation Act of that

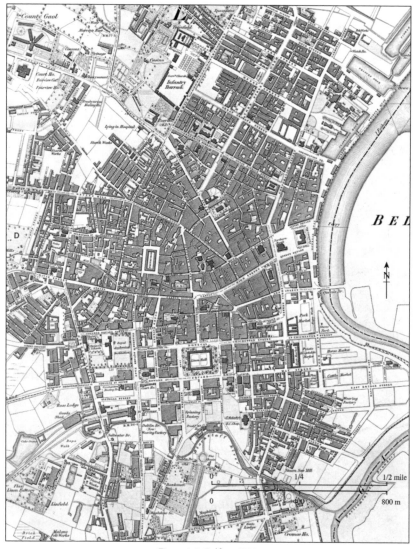

Figure 1.2 Belfast, 1858

year, which also raised the number of wards within Belfast from five to fifteen. Discussion on this act in the House of Commons veered off course and stimulated a debate on the non-representation of Catholics on the council. Edmund Vesey Knox, nationalist MP for Londonderry City, declared:

> The Catholics were ... almost one-fourth of the population, but yet they were not represented by even a single Member in the Corporation. This was not a chance matter ...[17]

However, the debate was brought back to the point by Sir James Haslett, Conservative MP for Belfast North (whose statue stands in the grounds of Belfast City Hall). Haslett stated:

> The Bill in its simplicity was a Bill simply to extend the borough of Belfast. That extension had been rendered necessary by the unprecedented growth of the city. It was not a question that the Corporation of Belfast had dealt lightly with or for Party purposes. It was a question forced upon them by the growth of the city.[18]

In 1898 the Local Government (Ireland) Act made Belfast a county borough and required annual elections for its lord mayor.

'The joyful acclamations of multitudes': The Donegalls' impact on Belfast
The rapid growth of Belfast, perhaps from the 1750s and certainly between the 1820s and the 1850s, can be at least partly ascribed to the ready availability of land. This was thanks to the complicated activities of the Chichester family, whose head, the earl, later the marquis of Donegall, was the sole landlord of the town. These men were descendants of Arthur Chichester, to whom Belfast had been granted by the crown in 1603. The Donegalls had a long tradition of making land available for public buildings in Belfast. Thus, in 1739, it was reported that the fourth earl 'hath been pleased to tend orders to several workmen here to draw up a plan of a linen hall ... and proposes to have such a one forthwith built at his own expense on the ground which his lordship lately caused to be wall'd in off the sea in Catherine Street'.[19] This would have been the Brown Linen Hall in Donegall Street. The family also contracted for St Anne's Church and the Assembly Rooms, the latter 'built and highly decorated at the sole expense of the [fifth] earl of Donegall' to celebrate the birth of his son and heir, George Augustus.[20] The chief expense of the fifth earl/first marquis was in funding the Lagan Navigation connecting Belfast by water to Lough Neagh. His obituary estimated expenditure on this to have been above £360,000.[21]

The Donegall family's influence on Belfast was not always benign, however. The fourth earl of Donegall, who inherited the title as a child in 1705, after his father died serving with the duke of Marlborough in Spain, has been regarded as weak minded. In 1754 he came close to being committed and, under his long period of nominal control of the Chichester estates, which included Belfast, there was little leadership and no programme of development for the town. Few leases had been issued before the trustees of the Donegall estate obtained a private act of parliament to enable them to do so. When these began to be released in the mid-1750s, they contained building or repairing clauses that led to improvements in the townscape. The fifth earl, a nephew of the childless incumbent, who inherited in 1757, took an active interest in the town and from 1765 clauses in the leases he issued helped to transform Belfast further. Raymond Gillespie, in the companion volume to this book, notes that different types of lease were issued. As well as leases for undeveloped land there were renewal leases, which required the property to be kept in good order, repairing leases, which required tenants to repair their properties, and building leases, which required that a property be demolished and rebuilt. Under the terms of this last type, restrictions could be and were imposed by the landlord to dictate the quality of building and thus the social geography of Belfast. High-status areas such as Castle Place had to have houses 28 feet (8.5 metres) high; the figure for High Street was 25 feet (7.6 metres); for Ann Street 18 feet (5.5 metres); cabins on Peter's Hill on the low-status western periphery had to be only 10 feet (3 metres) high. Gillespie points out that rebuilding clauses had most impact in the suburbs, which by the end of the eighteenth century would have made the entry into Belfast more salubrious than it had hitherto been.[22]

Following the burning down of Belfast Castle in 1708, which had killed several family members, the earls of Donegall had been absentee landlords. The appearance of the fifth earl in Belfast in 1765 was a remarkable event:

> Yesterday evening the Right Honourable the Earl of Donegall and his Lady arrived at his Lordship's house in this town … amidst the joyful acclamations of multitudes of his Lordship's tenants. On this happy occasion there were bonfires, illuminations, firing of great guns …

it is remarkable that his Lordship is the first of his noble family who hath been in the town of Belfast for upwards of sixty years.[23]

A few weeks later the countess of Donegall 'was pleased to give the Ladies and Gentlemen of the town and neighbourhood a ball at the Market House, which was by far the grandest, most numerous and brilliant that was ever in this place'.[24] The earl was rarely seen in the town again, using the income from his *c.* 250,000 acre (100,000 hectare) holdings in Ireland to build a Palladian mansion in Staffordshire with grounds by Capability Brown.[25] The fifth earl was aggrandised as the first marquis of Donegall in 1791.

The second marquis was not an absentee, living much of the time in Belfast in an often vain attempt to distance himself from his creditors in England. The second marquis was 'an overdrawn character, indeed, in every sense of the word', as his biographer has it, adding that 'from an early age he set out to spend his sober father's money recklessly on the turf and at the gaming table'.[26] By 1791, still in his early twenties, Lord Belfast, as he was then, had debts of some £30,000. Despite a complicated settlement from his father, he contracted further debts and the exasperated first marquis let him spend time in a debtor's prison. Edward May, later to become a Belfast MP, helped to get Lord Belfast out and he was persuaded, presumably in return, to marry Anna May, Edward's illegitimate daughter. This further displeased the first marquis and he settled all the property he could on his second son, Spencer Chichester. This property, which included Ballymacarrett on the County Down side of the river, passed through the Templemore title.

Lord Belfast, now with relatives to support, was soon back in debt. The first marquis died in 1799 and the new second marquis's creditors assumed that they would at last be paid from the still-substantial holdings his father had been obliged to settle on him by family agreements, which included Belfast. As a peer, the second marquis could not be arrested for debt, although property might be taken. He began to enquire about the possibilities of raising cash by renewing Belfast leases in return for fines (cash payments). Bill Maguire's biography of the second marquis goes into detail about the complexities of both his finances and the contemporary legal and financial world, detail that cannot be reproduced here. Suffice it to say that, in order to escape his creditors:

> Donegall decided – or much more likely was induced – to flee to Ireland. Such valuables as he had been able to retain or acquire were sent secretly to Belfast to avoid seizure by his creditors and the family followed shortly after.[27]

Lord Donegall, as he was by now known, remained in Belfast as that rare beast, a resident Irish landlord, which helped bring popularity to himself and his family. He headed charities and subscription lists for good causes and was described as the 'best of landlords' in 1829.[28] His grandson was a particular favourite in the community, perhaps because he supported worthy causes such as William O'Hanlon's campaign for better sanitation. O'Hanlon referred to him as 'that young Nobleman – an honour to his class – noble by rank, but still more so by personal worth and accomplishments – the Earl of Belfast'.[29] Lord Donegall lived initially on the corner of Donegall Place opposite the White Linen Hall, a building later to become the Royal Hotel. R.M. Young recalled, if perhaps not from personal experience:

> during the season – for Belfast had its own season – his splendid liveries might be seen driving up from the stables in Castle Lane. Two outriders preceded and two always followed the stately carriage with its four dashing horses.[30]

In 1807 Donegall moved out to a 200-acre (81-hectare) agricultural demesne at Ormeau, across the Lagan. He, his wife and their seven sons, together with an estimated forty servants, inhabited the pre-existing 'cottage' there for about twenty years. Creditors were constantly harassing Donegall, usually to little avail. His life was also complicated by a series of disputes regarding the validity of his marriage and, thus, the legitimacy of his children. This hinged not upon Anna May's age at marriage (although there were questions about whether she had been of full age), but about her illegitimacy – whether her father had had the right to give consent to the marriage or whether a legal guardian should have done so. If the marquis and marchioness of Donegall were not properly married, their seven sons were illegitimate, which would have considerable impact upon property and succession rights. In the event, an amendment to an act of 1753 legitimised the Donegalls' marriage on the grounds that it had been solemnised and they had continued to live together. This made Lord Belfast, the eldest son of the second marquis, legitimate once more. He could marry and his father could now settle Belfast upon him and raise the cash they both needed.

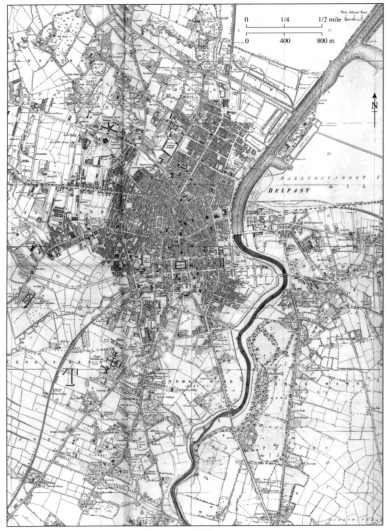

Figure 1.3 Belfast, 1860

The land was not sold outright; property prices were low in the 1820s given the depression that followed the end of the war with France. Maguire suggests that, anyway, Donegall would have wanted to keep the amount of money raised secret, which would not have been possible if it were sold. Rather, he let the plots of land (some of which he had earlier leased, usually for sixty-one years) on new perpetual leases of three lives (that is, the lifetimes of three nominated people) renewable forever on payment of a substantial lump sum in cash (the fine), as well as a modest, fixed, annual rent. The lessee could do what he liked with the land, even subletting it for others to develop, as long as the lives were renewed whenever necessary and the rent was paid. Donegall retained only mineral and water rights. Maguire comments that these perpetual leases were a principally Irish form of tenure that had largely been superseded by the nineteenth century. That they were revived for the sale of Belfast is a mark of how desperate the landowner was for ready cash, giving up all chance of increasing rents in the future in return for the fine, a one-off payment.

Six hundred Belfast leases were granted in the following ten years, mainly to industrialists and businessmen, with hundreds more leases granted in rural holdings in Counties Antrim and Donegal. Such was the scale of the transactions that printed *pro-forma* documents were made ready, with three of the Donegalls' sons already listed as the three lives. The sales of leases then stopped – according to Maguire, because Lord Belfast, characterised as 'careless' against his 'crafty' father, had become dissatisfied with what was happening, seeing his future income stream constantly sinking. The fines were supposed to be paid to an agent and, in theory, the Donegall family should have become free of debt, having raised perhaps over £300,000. However, this was not the case; there is some suggestion that Donegall himself took the money and continued in his irresponsible way. He built property in the country and kept a yacht, which he raced, presumably wagering upon the result. He also spent £86,000 on transforming Ormeau Cottage into the mock-Tudor mansion that was Ormeau House. The second marquis died in October 1844; shops and warehouses in Belfast closed for the morning of his funeral.[31]

At his death the second marquis's debts amounted to about £400,000. The third marquis was obliged to dispose of Belfast and

30,000 acres (12,100 hectares) in County Antrim through the Encumbered Estates Court to pay them off, although such had been the favourable terms of the leases issued by the second marquis that when his son tried to sell the land there was no rush to buy.[32] The third marquis died in 1883 and, as his own son was dead by then, the title went to an uncle and the property passed to his daughter, Harriet, who was married to the heir of the earl of Shaftesbury.

The second marquis of Donegall was 'charming', if 'weak and dim witted'.[33] He had some influence upon the town's politics, basically appointing its MPs prior to the Reform Act of 1832, usually to the benefit of his wife's family, the Mays, by whom he was ensnared. His most significant influence upon Belfast, however, was giving up control; issuing leases without restrictive covenants to the business class enabled the growing and rapidly industrialising town to develop without constraint. The Donegalls' problems had 'obliged the citizens to assert their independence of the landlord's control, which they were not in the least reluctant to do'. This helped to 'foster the climate of confident enterprise which prevailed in Victorian Belfast'.[34]

'A charnel house breaking in upon the gaiety and glitter of a bridal':
housing and socio-spatial patterns
Eighteenth-century Belfast had what might be recognised as a pre-industrial pattern to its social areas, with the wealthy tending to inhabit the centre of the town on the major streets and the poor the outskirts, although poor people could also be found in the back streets and alleys of the central town, especially once industrialisation had hit. Thus, in 1780 a visitor from Naas could write that he was:

> vastly surprised and hurt to see a long string of falling cabins and tattered houses, all tumbling down, with a horrid aspect, and the seeming prelude to a pitiful village, which was my idea of Belfast until I got pretty far into the town.[35]

The pattern and, indeed, the town changed. George Benn, in his notable history of 1823, was conscious of how rapidly the Belfast of his day was developing. Noting the 'fine shops with which [High Street] is entirely filled', he added that it was still 'only a very few years since the pedlars assembled here to sell their wares, as they do at present in the street of many a country town'.[36]

The field books from the 1837 valuation of Belfast record that Donegall Square West had 'the best situations in town as private residences. Very commodious and handsomely fitted out in every

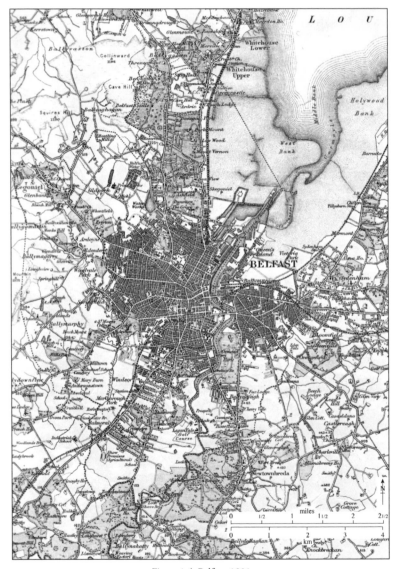

Figure 1.4 Belfast, 1901

way.'[37] But by mid-century 'southward, the suburban district is ... adapted for villa building, and around the Queen's College and Botanic Gardens new houses and streets of the best description are fast growing'.[38] Over a few decades the high-status residents of central Belfast moved away to such peripheral villas there or in outer east Belfast. One such was Gustavus Heyn, owner of a shipping company, who moved from Henry Street to Standtown House and then Bunker Hill in east Belfast in 1850. After Heyn, Bunker Hill was occupied in 1858 by Joseph Farren of the Eliza Street flax-spinning mill; in 1863 it was leased to David Corbett, who was also leaving Henry Street; and in 1873 by Alexander Forrester, a spirit merchant from Arthur Street who had lived above his shop. Nearby Ormiston House was inhabited by Sir Edward Harland and then, from 1887, by his Harland and Wolff partner William Pirrie. Some of the small estates were reused for institutional purposes later. For example, Purdysburn, the mental institution, was once the demesne of banker Narcissus Batt, who left it to hospital commissioners on his death in 1891.[39]

As Belfast developed, the town's middle class grew; industry, commerce and the public sector all provided opportunities for white-collar workers. Such people often took large terraced or semi-detached housing on the outskirts, often connecting to their employment in the centre of town by tram. One common type of red-brick, slate-roofed villa with bay windows from the late nineteenth and early twentieth centuries can still be found across what were then the city's outskirts in various guises as a terrace, a semi-detached pair or a detached house (Figure 1.5). Most Belfast housing was built of brick, much of it being manufactured from clay deposits within the town itself from an early period. Thus, in 1760, one James Young, brickmaker, had been ready to take orders for more than 50,000 bricks.[40] There were 20 different brick- and tile-making enterprises active up to 1840 and 137 in the period from 1840 to 1900.[41]

In other districts conditions were rather different: 'urbanisation had its bad side' is Alison Jordan's comment in her book on charity in Belfast. She goes on to note that the government's report on the state of the Irish poor in 1836 found that 'the condition of the poor in Belfast is, in some respects, superior to that of other towns'.[42] However, there were some descriptions of inferior conditions in the report and

Figure 1.5 Sandford Avenue

these related to places that had had the lowest valuations in 1837 – courts and alleys behind major streets such as High Street and Donegall Street. An evocative picture of real poverty and squalor in the midst of the expanding town in the mid-nineteenth century can be seen from the writings of two clergymen in the early 1850s. Reverend Anthony McIntyre's journal is a report to his employers, the Unitarian Domestic Mission to the Poor of Belfast, about how he dealt with people in his care. By contrast, Reverend William O'Hanlon's book was first published as a series of letters in the *Northern Whig* newspaper:

> Sir, Permit me to call the earnest attention of the more affluent, respectable and especially the Christian public of Belfast, to the deplorable condition of the poor who inhabit the back streets, courts and alleys of our rapidly extending and populous town.[43]

O'Hanlon was particularly struck by the spatial proximity but social gulf between those occupying the main streets and those in the back streets behind them; his simile was 'as a charnel house breaking in upon the gaiety and glitter of a bridal'. Table 1.1 and Figure 1.6 were compiled from the records of the visits by the two clergymen, which necessarily identified the poorest streets in Belfast. Many of these had been improved only a few years before, in 1849, when the council had ordered them to be cleansed and whitewashed[44] in order to reduce the incidence of fever.[45] In these areas lived many regularly employed industrial workers not in need of McIntyre's ministrations, but in their midst were people at the bottom of the socio-economic heap, usually without steady employment. McIntyre's report and O'Hanlon's book paint a bleak picture of the lifestyle and living conditions of such people, who survived often by casual home working, sewing especially, or by breaking stones. On occasion one or both of the clergymen would make a remark that characterised a street or court. These have been gathered together in Table 1.1.

Street	McIntyre	O'Hanlon
Anderson's Row		pleasing contrast
Barrack Lane		reeking feculence ... loathsome hovels
Bell's Lane	a very low place	
Brady's Row	so narrow	[bad] odour
Campbell's Court		refuse ... enough to poison
Caxton St	improper houses [brothels]	
Charlemont St	a most filthy street	
Chester Lane	poverty not to be described	
Davison's Court		cleanliness & beauty
Dickey's Entry		nuisances ... breed pestilence & death
Drummond's Court		conditions worse than beasts of the field
Grattan's Entry	not a good place	
Gratton Court	all manner of filth	
Gratton Place	all manner of filth	
Gregg's Lane	children run wild	
Hamill Street (court)		great dilapidation
Hudson's Entry	filthy place, houses of ill-fame [brothels]	den of vice & uncleanliness

Johnston's Court	so bad a place	
Jonney's Entry	most unwholesome, low, damp & confined	degrading & demoralising
Little Donegall St	wretched place	
Long Lane	two very bad houses [brothels]	
Lower Caxton St	bad houses [brothels], one of the worst parts	
Lower Kent St	much confined	
Lynas Court		nuisances … breed pestilence & death
McLean's Court		foul & filthy
McGrady's Entry		narrow & extremely filthy
McTier's Court		cockatrice's den
Meeting House Lane	dens of infamy [brothels]	
Morrison's Court		foul leprous den
Morrow's Entry	confined & filthy	
North St	upper part unwholesome	
North Queen St		facilities … for vice
Pepper Hill Court		laden atmosphere
Plunkett's Court		dark & filthy
Princes St	houses full of unfortunate females [brothels]	
Round Entry		loathsome corruption
Samuel St		atmosphere like a leaden weight
Sandy Row		suburban situation greatly in its favour
Smithfield		twenty public houses
Smithfield Court		scene of brawls
Stewart's Court		effluvium on the threshold
Suffern's Entry	a very bad place [brothels]	
Telfair's Entry	very unwholesome	
Upper Kent Street		like Tom All-alone's in Bleak House
Victoria Court		comparative refinement

Table 1.1. Comments by McIntyre and O'Hanlon, 1850s.

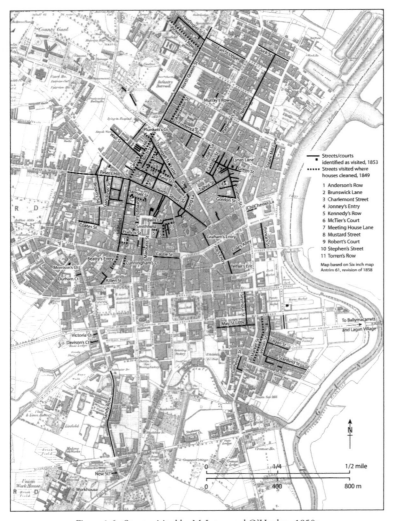

Figure 1.6   Streets visited by McIntyre and O'Hanlon, 1850s

The spatial pattern is clear from Figure 1.6; these poor people and their substandard housing were to be found behind the main streets of the northern part of central Belfast and in the Cromac area. Not all working-class housing was poor – Sandy Row was seen as suburban and salubrious despite its reputation as the haunt of the fiercest of the Protestant mobs. O'Hanlon described a development in Anderson's Row where carefully designed structures and a set of regulations agreed between tenants and landlord were conducive to good conditions and the 'houses are let as fast as they are built'.[46] Further, in Davison's Court off Durham Street, an enlightened and caring landlord worked with his tenants to produce 'little palaces for cleanliness and beauty'.[47] A factory, John Chartres and Company's Falls Mill, was singled out for providing its 800 or so workers with houses that were kept in 'admirable condition'. They were whitewashed regularly, had running water and were inspected once a month, yet cost the tenants no more than the usual rent for mill housing.[48] However, the people in these areas mostly lived lives blighted by poverty in dire conditions. Let just one detailed description from O'Hanlon stand duty for the scores of others:

> Plunging into the alleys and entries of this neighbourhood, what indescribable scenes of poverty, filth, and wretchedness everywhere meet the eye! Barrack-lane was surely built when it was imagined that the world would soon prove too strait for the number of its inhabitants. About five or six feet [1.5–1.8 metres] is the space here allotted for the passage of the dwellers, and for the pure breath of heaven to find access to their miserable abodes. But in truth, no pure breath of heaven ever enters here; it is tainted and loaded by the most noisome, reeking feculence, as it struggles to reach these loathsome hovels. These are, in general, tenanted by two families in each, and truly it is a marvel and a mystery how human beings can, in such a position, escape disease in its most aggravated and pestilential forms.[49]

O'Hanlon pressed for improvement:

> the chief desiderata are, improved drainage; more copious supplies of water; great attention to all that gives birth to malaria and animal poisons; the entire destruction of tenements where foul air, filth and disease cannot but dwell together and hold carnival.[50]

Almost twenty years later came a further dreadful account, in this case of Ballymacarrett. This was in a report to the council from Dr James Hill, medical officer for the Castlereagh Dispensary District, which included Ballymacarrett. Here low-lying parts were found to be flooded for much of the winter. Many dwellings were unfit for human habitation and knowledge of tide times was useful to Dr Hill when planning visits to some streets. 'It is high time that something should be done,' he thundered. The council intended to improve sanitation and sewerage east of the river, but funding was difficult.[51] Councillor Henry O'Neill admitted in 1901:

> Little, if any attention whatever was paid to sanitary matters until comparatively recent years, streets were laid out to suit the convenience of the owner of the ground and lanes and alleys were numerous in the immediate neighbourhoods of the widest and best streets of the city ... with a view to the housing of as many persons as possible, without caring whether there was sufficient air, proper ventilation, water, or any essentials for the health of the persons living therein.[52]

O'Neill added:

> there are still many lanes and alleys in the City which require considerable attention, but in the great majority of these little can be done, unless by the total removal of the houses and reconstruction of the streets.[53]

Such work was being carried out under the Housing of the Working Classes Acts (1885 onwards) and through the adoption of model building bye-laws.[54] Redevelopment and especially the building of new streets resulted in much of working-class Belfast becoming characterised by what Emrys Jones called 'endless rows of tiny kitchen houses'.[55] These houses could be erected for under £50 and their rental of two to three shillings per week placed them within the reach of the labouring classes.[56]

Housing for the industrial workers had become more mannered towards the end of the century, when speculative building provided dwellings in anticipation of demand, so these had to be reasonably attractive. One example would be McMaster Street off the Newtownards Road, permission for the building of which was granted by the council in 1897. It contained terraced houses, but with distinctive and contrasting brickwork around doors and windows, making this and other contemporary developments of its sort more distinguished than earlier Belfast terraces. McMaster Street was to become one of Belfast's conservation areas in 1994, chosen because it represented the best surviving example of late-Victorian terraced housing in the city (Figure 1.7).[57]

Figure 1.7 McMaster Street

Some of the most significant townscape developments of the era were in central Belfast – such as Victoria Street, where the town hall was erected in 1871. Another was the replacement of Hercules Street, an insalubrious area populated by butchers, by Royal Avenue. In 1864 the council considered a proposal to put a new, wide street through from Donegall Avenue to York Street, a development of grand proportions with an associated cost. A public company was formed to manage the project, for which an act of parliament would be necessary; the company applied to the council for a £15,000 subvention.[58] The following year the council minutes record that 'An Act to authorize the opening of certain new Streets in the Borough of Belfast, and to confer certain Powers upon a Company and the Mayor, Aldermen, and Burgesses of the Borough of Belfast' had been passed,[59] but it was only under the Belfast Improvement Act of 1878 that the work commenced. Royal Avenue was finished and named in 1881.[60]

A 'total inattention to cleanliness'
The gathering together of growing numbers of people in Belfast generated problems of cleanliness and waste disposal that blighted the

lives of the poor especially, but were hard for anybody to escape. In 1758 George Macartney, the sovereign (the equivalent of mayor), described the streets 'as in general being full of intolerable heaps of dirt' and begged that the owners of such heaps would remove them 'for their own and their neighbour's sakes' within a week. The composition of the heaps of dirt may be gauged by the fact that if they were not disposed of he would 'grant warrants to such as want dung' to help themselves to them.[61] A similar warning was issued by Macartney in 1764,[62] the same year that the local newspaper editorialised: 'what must strangers think of us whose streets are in many places in holes, and in some places almost impassable with dirt, dung and filth[?]'[63]

The sovereign made further remarks on townspeople who have 'neglected to sweep their streets [and] have suffered dung, dirt and other filth to be laid out and continued thereon' in 1776,[64] but rows of dung lined some streets still two years later.[65] In 1782 concerned citizens, presumably exasperated at the lack of progress, resolved that they would employ horses and carts themselves to carry away all dung and waste dumped on the street.[66] Presumably stung at this implication about his inability to enforce his own regulations, the sovereign himself was patrolling the streets a few weeks later, fining people who had contravened the rules. He vowed to do this twice a week until 'the inhabitants acquire a proper sense of the propriety of cleanliness in such a populous town'.[67] This initiative seems not to have become established practice, for a few years later there were again complaints about the 'total inattention to cleanliness' in Belfast, a problem that was not only 'injurious to the health' of townspeople, but also would give visitors a 'contemptible idea of the place', an important consideration in a town 'so rapidly improving in numbers, commerce and manufactures'.[68]

The sovereign was seeking a contract for the streets to be swept and the dirt carried away on Wednesdays and Saturdays in 1798.[69] Two years later came the Belfast Police Act of 1800, under which:

> all regulations ... respecting the paving, lighting and cleaning the streets; and every other circumstance conducive to the health or comfort of the inhabitants are under the government or superintendence of the police commissioners.[70]

The act specifically forbade people:

> to empty any night soil [faeces], ordure or filth from any sewer, privy or boghouse or other place on any street, lane or place within the said town, or throw from any door or window into the same any urine, ordure or filth.[71]

The penalty upon conviction was a fine of twenty shillings. In practical terms this act would seem to have made little difference. Street cleaning, still on Wednesdays and Saturdays, was contracted out and, even though there was regular inspection of the work during on-site visits by the police commissioners,[72] the system still did not keep Belfast clean. A dozen years on it was seen 'to rival Dublin itself in dirtiness'.[73] A few years later another police bill was passed to regularise the paving and cleaning of the streets further.[74] There was particular distress from one correspondent to the newspaper caused by the streets being filthy on the Sabbath.[75] The Police Committee advertised in 1820 for a contractor to sweep and cleanse the town, disposing of the heaps of manure,[76] but in 1823 came a report that:

> Every man looks as though he were dressed to perform the part of the Dusty Miller ... our streets are now so completely covered in dust, and our atmosphere so loaded with floating particles of horse dung, pulverised straw, stoney matter etc, etc, ground to atoms, that passengers in less than twenty minutes become masked with a compound powder which it would puzzle Sir Humphrey Davy to analyse ... clerks may tot up their accounts on their dusty counters with their middle finger.[77]

It was agreed that there was a need to water the streets to keep down the 'noxious floating filth' that blew into the shops, harming the goods and 'forming a fit nidus for moths'.[78] Shopkeepers and householders could be fined for not sweeping the pavement outside their shops before ten o'clock in the morning and nine shopkeepers were so punished in 1823.[79] However, some householders, rather than cleaning, just added to the problem – there was an 'intolerable nuisance' from water and refuse being thrown out of windows and doors.[80] At this time the graveyards were described as a 'receptacle of filth'.[81]

Animals were nuisances, too, whether they were alive, dead or dying. 'Allowing herds of swine to go through the streets unmolested' was a 'shameful defect';[82] and in 1793 townspeople were warned that all pigs found 'strolling through the streets and lanes' were to be slaughtered for the use of the poor.[83] Even if this threat was carried out, it did not solve the problem – two years later came the presumably ironic comment that 'the circumstance of allowing such a number of swine to run abroad is rather uncommon in so genteel and respectable place as Belfast'.[84] Livestock, including cattle, were killed in the streets, especially the shambles on Hercules Street, where the butchers congregated. The sovereign was determined to have this practice properly regulated in 1772,[85] but again to no avail. The 'persistent nuisance' of the shambles, it was later declared, 'would not only disgrace the least civilized country in Europe, but cannot fail to communicate sickness in every passing gale'.[86]

The regulations were not themselves without deleterious environmental outcomes. There is a report of an unwholesome carcase being condemned by the council and officially disposed of by being thrown into the dock.[87] Fever in Belfast in 1817 was thought to have been associated with this type of practice:

> the Police Committee [should] prevent the continued nuisances that are cast into and heaped up in May's Dock by the butchers, porters and others, which are in themselves sufficient to spread contagion, exclusive of stopping up the flowing and ebbing of the tide and obstructing the free passage of the sewers.[88]

Readers of O'Hanlon's *Walks among the poor of Belfast* will not need reminding that matters had not improved much, at least in the back lanes, by 1853. By way of example, one description from a large choice will be sufficient: there was a court off the top of Hamill Street where a dispute over ownership had led to it not being taken under council supervision. The result was that:

> a sea of stagnant water, mingled with refuse of every description, stretches not very sublimely all along the front of the dwellings – I should say stagnant except as it is ever and anon agitated by accumulations made to this horrible cesspool.[89]

As might be expected, Dr Andrew Malcolm's celebrated work on the sanitary state of Belfast expressed opinions on street cleaning. According to Malcolm:

> the removal of all vegetable and animal remains from the surface of our public ways is manifestly as important a sanitary procedure as the due efficiency of the public sewers.[90]

Whilst the condition of the main streets was acceptable to him, Malcolm identified problems regarding 'poorer localities', where the streets were largely unpaved, 3,000 houses were without yards and a much greater number were 'deficient in still more necessary accommodation'.[91] Improvements later in the period can be traced through Councillor O'Neill's article, mentioned above.[92]

'Nothing short of the railway car and the electric telegraph will suffice': infrastructure

Filling 'banks with right good will': rivers, water and bridges
Belfast's earliest piped water supply, using wooden pipes (Figure 1.8), was established in 1678 and in the eighteenth century the system was in the hands of George Macartney. In 1733 the earl of Donegall leased rights to the waters of all courses not already in Macartney's hands to William Johnston of Newforge. In his history of Belfast's water supply, Jack Loudan pointed out that 'Pipe-Water' Johnston, as he had become known, seems to have made little profit from his venture and he offered his lease to others in 1753.[93] In 1755, then, it was one Lewis Jones who informed customers of his water-supply business through a notice in the newspaper that some of them were in arrears, whilst he had employed Archibald Henning, pump and pipe borer, to work on the waterworks.[94] A successor, James Hall, declared in 1762 that under his stewardship the system was in much better order and repair than hitherto and that it was now necessary to 'seek a great advance on the present low rent' charged to customers.[95]

The water came from low-level springs feeding a milldam south of Belfast, entering the town at Donegall Pass, where a small reservoir

WOODEN WATER PIPE
LAID IN BELFAST 1733-1750
FOUND IN BRIDGE ST.WIDENING 1956

Figure 1.8 Wooden water pipe

had been constructed.[96] Hall also sold water from barrels mounted on carts, some people preferring that to the piped water, which was thought to be injurious to health. Water that came from the wells at Cromac had a particular reputation for 'purity and agreeability'.[97] Such was the demand for Cromac water that the horses drawing the carts were worked for eighteen hours a day. Newspaper reports complained of their poor condition and ill treatment, claiming that they suffered from excessive use of the whip.[98]

As Belfast grew, Hall's wooden pipes and carts were unable to provide a supply that could equal demand. A new supplier came in 1795, when 'the people of Belfast found themselves in the unusual position of having water supplied to them by the Poorhouse authorities'.[99] The Poor House in Clifton Street was being developed in the early 1770s and had struggled to find a supply of water for its own operation. The Belfast Charitable Society, which ran the Poor House, developed the idea of becoming involved in water supply itself.

This would have the dual benefits of securing an income and improving living conditions in Belfast. In 1784 the committee of the Belfast Charitable Society met to consider the idea of purchasing the system[100] and in 1795 the marquis of Donegall granted the society a sixty-one-year lease 'of certain springs and fountains of water' near Belfast 'for the purpose of supplying the inhabitants ... with pure and wholesome water'.[101] The *Belfast News Letter* thanked his lordship.[102] At first much of the distribution was limited to water carts: 'a car goes round the town every day with Poor-house water for sale at the rate of a halfpenny per measure of four gallons'.[103]

The old wooden pipes were subject to rot, frost in winter caused interruptions to supplies and illness was being attributed to the impure state of water in the town.[104] In 1795 the Belfast Charitable Society employed an Edinburgh engineer, James Gordon, to advise them on water supply. The society set up the Spring Water Commissioners to manage supplies from a number of local sources, a scheme 'highly approved of' by the newspaper, which noted that the springs formerly used 'have been so ill-managed that not half of their produce reached the town'.[105] Even so, development was slow; the poor were distressed because there were insufficient cocks at the public fountain in 1801 and, the next year, were described as being 'very badly off' for water, that 'useful article'.[106] By 1810 matters seemed to have improved – it was reported that, despite a drought of some weeks, there had been abundant supplies from the reservoir:

> for this we are indebted to the genius and exertions of a respectable townsman who projected and superintended the additional supply ... only a third of the quantity that the springs will afford has yet been conducted to the town.[107]

However, fifteen years later, even though by then George Benn had noted that most pipes were metal, the supply–demand equation had once more become unbalanced. There were complaints that supplies might be interrupted for up to three days at a time,[108] but matters were eased by a programme of repairs, the replacement of existing pipes and an extension of the network.[109]

By 1840, the Belfast Charitable Society's control of the water supply had been questioned for some time. The Belfast Water Act of that year

Figure 1.9 Seal of the Belfast
Water Commissioners

passed responsibility to a new body, the Belfast Water Commissioners (Figure 1.9). The Belfast Charitable Society met formally in the Poor House to take this bill into consideration and were later compensated by the guarantee of a free supply and an annuity of £800.[110]

The Belfast Water Commissioners soon sought new sources of supply in addition to their inherited sources at Lyster's Dam, Malone, which fed a service reservoir at Basin Lane and provided supply through the pipes to public fountains in most cases. There were also springs at Lisburn Road and Sandy Row. The local newspaper had been reporting on searches for new sources of water even before the Water Act[111] and the Belfast Water Commissioners constructed basins on the Antrim Road, supplied by springs on Cave Hill, and a reservoir at Carr's Glen, although competition from mill owners for water from this source led to legal battles lasting a number of years. By March 1842 the reservoir was nearly complete and the cast-iron pipes for conveying the water were being delivered.[112] A few months later the Belfast Water Commissioners were ready to supply all dwelling houses that had been connected.[113]

However, Dr Andrew Malcolm observed in 1852 that about 7,000 of Belfast's 10,000 houses were served from the twenty-four public fountains, pumps sunk by landlords or water carts, whilst 'rain water is also sedulously collected by almost all families for washing and other domestic purposes'.[114] In 1855 a consultant water engineer, John Frederick Bateman, reported to the Water Commissioners that the present supply from the waterworks was 455,040 gallons per day, which, if the system were improved as recommended by the ubiquitous architect and engineer Charles Lanyon, could be increased to 1,044,000 gallons per day. However, in 1852 Bateman had estimated the need to be 2,000,000 gallons each day:

there is scarcely any town in the kingdom where the population is increasing at so rapid a rate in proportion to its size; nor where a deficient supply of water for the various increasing mercantile establishments of the place would be more severely felt.[115]

He recommended a scheme using the River Woodburn towards Carrickfergus in association with other sources. Nothing happened very speedily and by 1865 the situation was in crisis once again. Then the railway and civil engineer William Dargan, perhaps more noted for other works in Belfast, was finally engaged to build the new reservoirs at Woodburn, which eased the situation for another few years. Another water act in 1874 enabled the Woodburn scheme to be expanded; an 1884 act saw reservoirs constructed at Stoneyford towards Lisburn, extended in 1889. There were still problems over the volume and quality of supply, demonstrated by a typhoid outbreak in 1898.

It was clear that a groundbreaking scheme was needed to secure a long-term supply of fresh water for the industrial city. Lough Neagh was mentioned but its water was not of good quality and there was a problem with its height and the consequent need for pumping at considerable cost. Loudan's book details a number of other locations that were considered for a substantial reservoir for Belfast – a site near Ballynahinch, Slieve Croob, the Upper Bann, Bryansford, Clady, Glenravel, Glenarm – but for all of these there were problems of scale or cost or competition or quality. Finally, in the Mourne Mountains the Belfast Water Commissioners' engineer, Luke Livingstone Macassey, found a pure source of water at the manageable height of 2,500 feet (762 metres). Rights to the water were granted by the Belfast Water Act of 1893. Initially, river water from the Mournes supplied Belfast in connection with a storage reservoir at Knockbracken, but to secure supply in 1923 a dam across the Silent Valley was begun. It was finished in 1933.[116]

Supplying drinking water was not the only problem Belfast had with water at this period; the settlement was troubled by the Blackstaff River. O'Hanlon ironically compared Cambridge University and the Cam to Queen's College and the Blackstaff:

> [the river] fills its banks with right good-will, and contains the largest possible amount of matter [i.e. rubbish] within the smallest possible space – in this last particular affording a practical solution of a great problem which has long puzzled the wisest mathematicians.[117]

When near the Blackstaff, O'Hanlon felt himself 'as though actually pursued by grim pestilence and death'.[118] Such a situation was caused by sewage, industrial effluent and household waste and gave rise to the term the 'Blackstaff Nuisance'.

Another problem was flooding. Des O'Reilly, in his book on Belfast rivers, notes that flooding took place in 1796, 1838, 1868 and 1869, with conditions worsened by the removal of vegetation in the area, which had increased runoff.[119] A major attempt to ease matters came in 1887 when the Blackstaff was culverted from Great Victoria Street to the Gas Works, but this did not solve the problem and between 1906 and 1921 there were 101 separate floods. Increased and improved management of the river basin in the twentieth century eased the situation but did not solve it, given the problems for drainage caused by the low-lying position of the city of Belfast.

The junction of the Rivers Farset and Lagan had provided the advantages that had led to the settlement's original development. However, rivers need to be bridged. The first bridge across the Lagan within Belfast was the Long Bridge, built in 1685, with its twenty-one arches. Its County Down landing was damaged by storm in 1772 and it was recognised that it needed speedy repair;[120] however, the structure became increasingly difficult to maintain in good condition. By the early nineteenth century the Long Bridge was handicapping the development of Belfast – its narrowness impeded the passage of the many people who needed to cross the river. Another bridge was erected in 1809. This was Ormeau Bridge in south Belfast, but it collapsed shortly after being opened, being rebuilt in 1812–14.[121]

In 1812 the Long Bridge was declared capable of being repaired once more, so a plan to build a direct replacement for it was shelved,[122] although seven years later a report concluded that all twenty-one of the Long Bridge's arches needed attention and twelve were positively dangerous.[123] In 1821 it was resolved to repair the Long Bridge again and also to increase its capacity by adding a footpath, but the following year came the suggestion, again, that a new bridge should replace it.[124] This stimulated newspaper discussion, with one correspondent asserting that the Long Bridge 'will outlast that shameful modern structure, the Ormeau Bridge, which was a gross job'.[125] More years passed until in 1829 it was once more declared that the Long Bridge was in a dangerous state.[126] Plans for replacing it were announced in 1836,[127] a few months before some of its breastwork fell into the Lagan.[128] The design of the replacement, Queen's Bridge, by Charles Lanyon, was revealed in 1838,[129] and builders were called for to erect it in 1840.[130] Queen's Bridge opened later that year, twenty-eight years after discussions on the need to replace the Long Bridge had started.[131]

In 1844 the council were seeking to improve the approaches to Lanyon's bridge,[132] but at least the structure by Belfast's principal architect did not fall down, unlike those built before and, indeed, after it. This third crossing of the Lagan at Belfast in the Victorian period was the Lagan Bridge, positioned between the other two. Opening in 1848 and later renamed the Albert Bridge, in 1886 it also collapsed. A temporary pontoon bridge had to serve until it was repaired.[133] The Albert Bridge reopened in 1890.[134]

'Praying aid' and a 'famous engineer': harbour developments to c. 1850
In eighteenth-century Belfast the provision of quays was largely a matter for merchants. Hanover Quay was erected by Isaac McCartney between 1716 and 1720 and reclaimed the strand between the mouth of the Farset and the Long Bridge, taking quays onto the banks of the Lagan for the first time.[135] Thus began a long process of managing the Lagan and reclaiming land from its lower reaches; in 1791 a further embankment south of the Long Bridge on part of the Short Strand 'was closed, so as to exclude the tide'.[136] Hanover Quay sufficed until 1769, when Thomas Greg leased McCartney's quays and also built Chichester Quay on the north bank of the Farset, so named to celebrate the safe delivery of a child to the fifth earl of Donegall and his wife.[137] (This baby would become the second marquis of Donegall.)

A related issue was the difficult access into the port area from Belfast Lough. In 1785 a town meeting had decided to petition the newly independent Irish parliament, 'praying aid' for straightening and deepening the channel from the quaysides of central Belfast to the pool of Garmoyle further into Belfast Lough. Here large ships had to offload into lighters or at least lighten load and wait for high tide before proceeding into Belfast at considerable cost and inconvenience.[138] No grant was forthcoming, but an important change took place. An act was passed that transferred responsibility for control of the harbour from the town's corporation to a new body, the Corporation for Preserving and Improving the Port of Belfast, usually known as the Ballast Board. Fifteen commissioners were appointed; three were figureheads, including the earl of Donegall; the other twelve, who carried out the work, were Belfast merchants. They improved the channel to the lough, marked its course and also employed William Ritchie, who had recently begun to build ships in Belfast, to embank land north of the Farset. Ritchie built the first of the two Corporation (dry) Docks there, which opened in 1800. Private merchants also built quays, including Narcisus Batt, who built a quay on the County Down side in 1794 and Henry Joy Tomb, who built Donegall Quay, north of Waring Street. Dunbar's Dock was built in 1831. The second and longer of the two Corporation Docks had been built in 1826 (see Figure 1.1).[139]

The need for improved access still remained and a number of expensive proposals were made after 1814 involving notable engineers such as Sir John Rennie and Thomas Telford, although they were not put into operation.[140] However, in 1830 a scheme commissioned from James Walker of London for cuts to be made through the final two bends of the Lagan, providing an easy, deep-water approach to the port, was accepted: the Act for the Further Improvement of the Port and Harbour of Belfast in Ireland and for Other Purposes was passed in 1831. In 1832 the government agreed to advance £30,000.[141] This scheme was controversial; the marquis of Donegall objected and the cost of obtaining some necessary land was prohibitive. Further, Lord Templemore, who owned Ballymacarrett, put forward proposals of his own to develop a port on his (County Down) bank of the Lagan. All this occasioned delay and it was not until 1837 that the board was authorised to begin under the Act for the Formation of a New Cut or Channel and for Otherwise Improving More Effectually the Port and Harbour of Belfast, which repealed the 1831 act.

William Dargan of Carlow was engaged – a 'famous engineer and builder of Irish railways, promoter of the Great Exhibition 1853', as his memorial plaque at Carlow Station has it (Figure 1.10). Significantly, Dargan also had experience of building canals in Ireland. He commenced work on the first cut in 1839 and the spoil was dumped on its eastern side to form Dargan's Island, later renamed Queen's

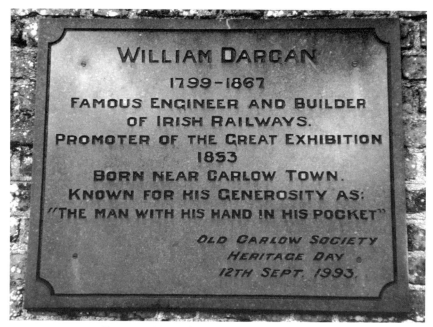

Figure 1.10 Memorial to William Dargan, Carlow Station

Figure 1.11 Customs House

Island, which became a pleasure ground before becoming a major site for shipbuilding. The Ballast Board bought all private quays in 1845 and within a few years had built berths on the County Down side as well as constructing a continuous line of quays on the County Antrim shore. In 1847, the Belfast Harbour Commissioners, as the old Ballast Board had become, commissioned the second cut, partly to provide work during the famine. Dargan again supervised the project. It was opened for traffic in 1849, when the Victoria Channel provided straight deep-water access into Belfast (see Figures 1.3 and 1.4). The final touches were the construction of the Graving Dock Basin (Clarendon Dock) near the Corporation Docks, which necessitated the relocation of shipbuilding facilities to a patent slip on Queen's Island. The infilling of areas behind the quays provided a cargo-handling area and the development of Victoria Street, leading from Corporation Street into the centre, meant better communication with the town. The Harbour Commissioners built themselves a new office on a former shipyard site near Clarendon Dock. Designed in-house by George Smith, it opened in 1854. Three years later came the splendid new Customs House by Charles Lanyon, which was erected on the nearby site of the old Ballast Board offices.[142]

Later in the century quays and docks, especially on the County Antrim shore, were extended for commercial use: the Spencer and Dufferin Docks (1872), Albert Quay (1875) and York Dock, behind Albert Quay (1889–97). Donegall Quay and Prince's Quay were reconstructed, timber being replaced by masonry by 1888. The Victoria Channel was deepened and extended. Once all the land around the Victoria Channel had been reclaimed and used, there was a need for further water frontage and between 1899 and 1903 the Musgrave Channel was built south of Queen's Island. Once again, the spoil from the dredging work was used to reclaim land. (The third, northern, prong of the familiar trident-shaped port of Belfast, the Herdman Channel and the associated Pollock Docks, was built in 1930; its spoil was used to extend the shore at Sydenham where Short Brothers (Bombardier) and what is now the George Best Belfast City Airport were located.) A commentary on later harbour developments regarding shipbuilding facilities can be found in the next chapter.

'Time is so precious now': communications

The Victorian era was one of rapid development in terms of communications. O'Hanlon noted:

> our forefathers found the sober stage coach and the ordinary post sufficiently rapid for all their purposes, but nothing short of the railway car and the electric telegraph will suffice to meet the demands of our existing social economy. Time is so precious now.[143]

Within Belfast, trams became a means of saving some of this precious time. The first mention of trams came in 1858, when the council denied an application to build a line to transport goods from the Ulster Railway terminus to the docks. This was rejected because the streets across which the tramway would have run were thought to be too busy. However, the establishment of a general system of horse tramways was under consideration in 1871.[144] The end of the nineteenth century was an era in which cities and even small towns in Britain and Ireland set up or took control of many functions that would later be run by private companies. Belfast was no exception, and the council petitioned unsuccessfully against the Belfast Street Tramways Bill in 1872, wishing this to be a municipal venture.[145] The Belfast Street Tramways Company was founded under the bill. A little later permission was granted to conduct trials of steam-powered trams,[146] but these cannot have been a success as the council forbade the use of anything other than animal power to propel trams in 1884.[147] The corporation still wished to control the tram service and attempted to buy out the company in 1902, finally succeeding in 1904 with the passing of the Belfast (Tramways) Act. The corporation immediately made plans to transfer to electric power, a major operation which took ten months, during which time 500 horses continued to provide power. On 5 December 1905, 'without a hitch … 174 [electric] cars were put into service in one single night'.[148]

Regarding the other form of tracked transport, railways, a company to finance a line from Belfast to Lisburn was being set up in 1825,[149] although George Stephenson's plans for this, the Ulster Railway (later the Great Northern Railway), were only delivered in 1837.[150] The line opened in 1839, with the terminus in Great Victoria Street.[151] There were other ventures. Shares for a railway running between Belfast and Holywood were issued in 1837;[152] it was agreed later that the system was to incorporate Comber and Newtownards.[153] This was the Belfast and County Down Railway, which opened in 1848, with its terminus east of the river. The Belfast to Ballymena railway prospectus was issued in 1844.[154] This line, the Belfast and Northern Counties Railway, also opened in 1848, with the terminus in York Road. The three railways had suburban stations, which assisted the growth of Belfast by facilitating commuting. Another company, the Belfast Central Railway, linked the termini by 1878 but it went bankrupt and had to be taken over by the Great Northern Railway in 1885.[155] A different type of enterprise was the single track from Cave Hill down to the docks to transport limestone from the quarries there. This was to be used as profitable ballast for ships that had brought coal into Belfast as well as to supply local needs for roadmaking, building and, given the purity of the rock, agricultural purposes. Coal could be brought back from the harbour to 'supply several of the great commercial manufacturing establishments which are very convenient to the foot of the Cave Hill', if a branch line were to be built.[156] The line of this railway was marked on the map in 1833 but it did not open until 1840.[157]

O'Hanlon mentioned another technological evolution in Belfast, the electric telegraph. The erection of telegraph wires in Belfast had been proposed by a Glasgow company in 1863, to be carried on neat iron posts on the roofs of houses;[158] the first free-standing telegraph pole was recorded in 1865 at Queen's Bridge.[159] Police stations were certainly connected. The council discontinued the original system in 1869, when links were to be established between Belfast and coastal towns to the north.[160] Later, regarding the new technology of telephones, the Linen Merchants' Association published a list of towns with numbers of subscribers; if set against contemporary population totals Belfast had fewer people per telephone line than the average (Table 1.2). Perhaps this was a measure of Belfast's industrial significance, since it can be assumed that the majority of subscribers at this early period would have been businesses.

The Linen Merchants' Association in 1892 looked forward to 'telephonic communication' with Dublin and intervening towns, especially as the system employed would enable the voice to be

Settlement	Telephone subscribers (1887)	Population (1891)	People per subscription
Dewsbury	123	29,847	243
Bradford	545	216,361	397
Glasgow	1,202	658,073	547
Belfast	**419**	**255,950**	**611**
Nottingham	308	213,877	694
Edinburgh	363	269,407	742
Leeds	461	367,505	797
Birmingham	469	478,113	1,019
Huddersfield	81	95,420	1,178
Wakefield	17	23,315	1,371
Average			*654*

Source: adapted from Annual Report of the Linen Merchants' Association 1887, PRONI, D2088/11/2.

Table 1.2. Telephone subscribers 1887.

'conveyed with a distinctness hitherto unattained'.[161] By 1898 there were over 1,150 telephone lines in the city; there were 1,688 the following year.[162]

'Mild radiance': street lighting

A contract for lighting Belfast was advertised in 1757[163] and four years later a town meeting of persons occupying property worth five pounds *per annum* was called to see how best to put into operation a new act of parliament 'for enlightening the several cities … of this kingdom'.[164] The next year the sovereign called a meeting at the Market House to seek to raise money through voluntary subscription to light the town with oil lamps.[165] The *Belfast News Letter* began to campaign for proper lighting, telling of a man who had had his knee dislocated by a plank laid across a cart that had struck him in the dark; of another who had stumbled into the river; of robberies. It was 'necessary to have the town well lighted with lamps; which might be done at no great expense, as a great many are now lying by unused'.[166] A generation later the same newspaper complained of lamps being 'so ill-lighted that at twelve o'clock they give very little light, and one or two are almost totally extinguished'. Another issue was vandalism – 'disorderly persons' broke several lamps in 1773.[167] After the 1800 Police Act, lighting Belfast was one of the responsibilities of the Police Committee. The Police

Committee wished to have 700 lamps[168] – a considerable increase, for in 1798 a contract had been sought for only 366 lamps.[169] Lighting these lamps was a skilled job; seven 'active, well-behaved, steady men' were sought for the task in 1817 at the decent wage of twelve shillings and sixpence per week – considerably in excess of that on offer to sweepers and labourers, who were to receive only eight shillings.[170]

A contract for lighting the town with gas for a period of twenty-one years was signed by the Commissioners of Police in December 1821.[171] The streets to be illuminated were Church Lane, Ann Street, Long Bridge, Cornmarket, Castle Street, Donegall Place, High Street, Skipper Street, Bridge Street, Waring Street, Donegall Street and North Street.[172] Eighteen months later 'immense multitudes of people assembled to witness the lighting of our streets with gas and were highly gratified by the mild radiance',[173] although soon afterwards the gas lamps on the Long Bridge were destroyed by vandals.[174] The contract was transferred to the Gas Company in 1826, when shares were issued to raise capital. The prospectus claimed the Gas Works to be 'as handsome and perfect as any in the United Kingdom' and, with prescience, 'adequate for the supply of almost any additional demand which may arise from the rapid increase of the town, and extension of its manufacturing interests'.[175] As Belfast grew, new districts would be brought into the areas 'lighted and watched', as recorded in the corporation minutes. For example, in June 1844, after listing the streets to be lit, the council authorised the surveyor of works to prepare an estimate for the lamps required. There were 1,269 lamps by 1856 and 6,500 by 1893.[176]

The council first discussed the idea of taking the gas supply into public ownership in 1865, tempted by the profits.[177] There was also a problem with the quality of supply. The Police Committee's gas inspector noted in 1872 that the council was paying a lot for a supply of poor quality at variable pressure to lamps that were set further apart than in most other places.[178] The council purchased the Gas Company in 1873 and in the following year the minutes recorded, presumably with satisfaction, that the council had been buying superior coal and thus the quality of the gas produced for Belfast had improved.[179] In 1878 the Gas Committee ruled against electric lighting being provided,[180] but it soon became clear that electric light was an inevitability. The council, having made some preparations, set up the Electric Committee in 1894 and began discussions about a power station in Chapel Lane, with electricity being supplied for the first time in January 1895.[181] Shortly afterwards, arrangements had to be set in place for a new electric-light station. A site on the river was considered in 1896.[182] The corporation's electric-light station opened on East Bridge Street in 1898.[183]

'The shallow bed of death'

Nineteenth-century Belfast rapidly outgrew some of its earlier infrastructure, including its graveyards. The churchyard around the original parish church in High Street (where St George's Church was built in 1816) had become a nuisance, not least because it was occasionally flooded. The Belfast Police Act of 1800 forbade any further burials there, directing interments to the New Burying Ground near the Poor House (Clifton Street Cemetery),[184] which had been opened by (and became a source of income for) the Belfast Charitable Society in 1797.[185] What became illegal burials in the old churchyard were subject to massive fines: £35 for the person who actually dug a grave and £320 for the person who had ordered it done.[186] By 1818, however, there was no longer enough space in Clifton Street. The Parish Vestry acknowledged the 'offensive appearance' of Belfast's graveyards and an extensive plot alongside Clifton Street graveyard was purchased, to be walled in preparation for use.[187] Malcolm described the cemetery as being 'preserved in very excellent order' in 1852.[188]

Matters remained troublesome elsewhere, however. By 1824, the Catholic cemetery at Friar's Bush in Stranmillis had:

> barely enough soil sufficient to cover the coffin lids, and scarcely are the deceased deposited in the slight and shallow bed of death till they are devoured by the myriads of rats that have fattened and multiplied beyond calculation on human flesh.[189]

The very air in the local area was 'injurious due to decomposition'.[190] The second marquis of Donegall granted an extra acre to Friar's Bush in 1828 and the entire cemetery was consecrated by the bishop of Down and Connor the following year for the exclusive use of Catholics.[191] This was not a long-term solution, for in 1863 the council minutes recorded that bodies were 'deposited' at Friar's Bush rather than buried – a significant distinction – and old coffins were being dug up and burnt to make room for fresh depositions.[192]

Further capacity for Catholics was urgently required, but also for paupers. A town meeting in 1847 had discussed the need to provide a place of interment for poor persons dying in Belfast.[193] Eventually, in 1865, the council purchased land for a substantial new graveyard on the Falls Road.[194] The development of this site, to be called the Belfast Cemetery, was enabled by the Belfast Burial Ground Act of 1866 and the cemetery opened in 1869. Proprietary plots could be purchased, the costs varying with location; monuments and markers could be erected; and some land was set aside for the burial of paupers in unmarked graves.[195] This cemetery was supposed to cater for all denominations: there were separate areas for Catholics and Protestants and, from 1871, a small Jewish strip. However, there were problems about the proper exercise of control over the designated Catholic section and the Catholic Church purchased land on the other side of Falls Park called Milltown Cemetery to use instead. This saw the closure of the Catholic cemetery at Friar's Bush in 1869 for everyone except families with burial rights. The Catholic area of Belfast Cemetery was reallocated for Protestant use, with compensation paid to the Catholic Church. With the opening of these new burial grounds, portions of Clifton Street and Friar's Bush Cemeteries were closed. By 1910 further capacity was needed and it was necessary to instigate a compulsory purchase of 54 acres (22 hectares) of land adjoining Belfast Cemetery to its west – the Glenalina extension – which had been the site of a linen-beetling mill. The extended graveyard was renamed Belfast City Cemetery in 1913; the new section opened in 1915. The corporation also had to take land for burials outside the city, purchasing 45 acres (18 hectares) at Ballymiscaw, Dundonald, in 1899. The first burial took place there in 1905. Finally, the boundary extension of 1896 brought the ancient Knock Cemetery into Belfast, although no new burial plots were ever issued there.[196]

Parks for Belfast's 'soiled and alley-living population'
Dr Andrew Malcolm identified a pressing need for parks and open spaces in Belfast in 1852:

Belfast is sadly deficient in one of the most important requisites for
the health and comfort of a town population – we mean public parks
and pleasure grounds. We can point to only two squares of any
magnitude which are used as promenades. Our beautiful Botanic
Garden is not accessible to the masses of the community … were it

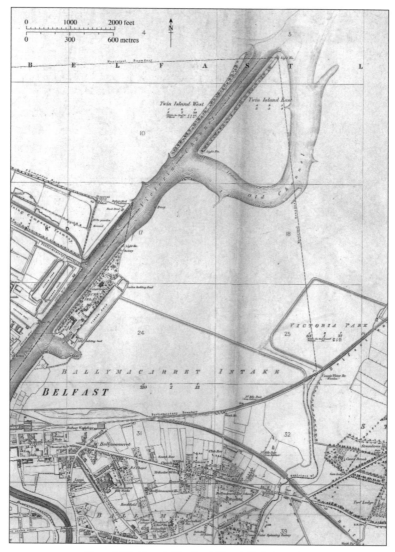

Figure 1.12 Queen's Island and Victoria Park site, 1860

not for the excellence of our public roads and the recent construction of an ornamental island in our harbour ... the greater proportion of the class referred to would be denied the use of free open-air recreation. The Queen's Island has, indeed, become a boon.[197]

Queen's Island was Dargan's Island, renamed for Queen Victoria's 1849 visit. It had been landscaped by the Harbour Commissioners and became the site of organised fêtes between 1850 and 1852. A permanent structure, the Crystal Palace, was erected in 1851. The island, commonly referred to as the People's Park, remained a place of resort even after the Crystal Palace itself burnt down in 1864.[198] It was always thought that Queen's Island would be needed for industry or docks and its leisure facilities were slated to be replaced by a 50-acre (20-hectare) site at the mouth of the Connswater in east Belfast, to be known as Victoria Park (Figure 1.12). This project had been mentioned as early as 1854 under the Belfast Dock Act and the land was drained in preparation but no further progress was made.[199] Harland and Wolff acquired the People's Park site between 1877 and

Figure 1.13 Palm House, Botanic Gardens

1879, but Victoria Park did not open until 1906. It rapidly became also a location for sports, including swimming.[200]

The other open space mentioned by Malcolm was the Botanic Gardens, a private venture of the Belfast Botanical and Horticultural Society dating to 1828.[201] In 1840 the society met in the Exchange Rooms to report that 'a large and splendid greenhouse' was in course of being built (Figure 1.13).[202] The gardens themselves were private, restricted to members or to visitors who could afford to pay the entrance charge, but as a gesture in 1840 the committee decided to admit the working classes each Saturday evening in June at a reduced price of twopence each.[203]

Others joined Malcolm in seeking an extension to the provision of open space in Belfast in the middle of the nineteenth century. James Thomson spoke to the Belfast Social Inquiry Society in 1852 on the need for parks in large towns and concluded with a specific plea that they should be provided in Belfast.[204] William O'Hanlon, in his campaign for better living conditions for the poor of Belfast, added:

> Is Belfast with its 104,000 inhabitants not able or willing to provide a park for its soiled and alley-living population to which they might be won and where they might learn the value of God's sunshine and air, and get a glimpse of nature in her genial and soul-reviving forms[?][205]

Later in the book he noted, regarding parks, that 'no place can be in greater need of such an outlet for a dense, toil-worn, sickly and miasm[a]-breathing population'.[206] Such pleas were not rapidly acted upon and, in his research on Belfast parks, Robert Scott found no reference to the corporation contemplating action until 1865. It was only in 1869 that a committee was formed, which could take action after the passing of the Public Parks (Ireland) Act of 1869. Immediately the corporation entered into negotiations with the marquis of Donegall to purchase his demesne at Ormeau and to obtain some of the land planned for the cemetery on Falls Road. The cost of Ormeau was met by allowing 40 acres (16 hectares) of the 175-acre (71-hectare) demesne to be used for building: North and South Parade resulted from this. The park was opened in 1871 with a parade, although landscaping and the addition of sporting facilities continued to be

Figure 1.14 Dunville Park

added for many years afterwards. Ormeau Golf Club was founded there in 1892 on a parcel of land that had previously been rented out for grazing. Some of the land at Falls Road was developed later – being outside the boundary of the town, the 1869 act did not apply to this land and it had to await enabling legislation in 1872. Falls Park opened in 1876.[207]

Other parks followed. Woodville (later Woodvale) Park, for example, was announced by the council in 1887 and opened in 1888.[208] Alexandra Park in north Belfast had been opened the previous year. Dunville Park on the Grosvenor Road, a gift to the new city from the distiller Robert Dunville, opened in 1892 (Figure 1.14). Finally, the council planned to acquire Botanic Gardens as a public park in 1893.[209] The practice whereby employers bought admission for their workforces had helped with funding and further income had come from the gardens being let for meetings and entertainment – Blondin, the famous tightrope walker, appeared and balloon flights took place. The Royal Belfast Botanic and Horticultural Company was able to finance new facilities, including the Tropical Ravine of 1887, but ran into difficulties even so. The Royal Belfast Botanic Garden was sold to the corporation for £10,500[210] and was opened as the Belfast Botanic Gardens Park on 1 January 1895.[211] Another open space used for recreation was the reservoir site on the Antrim Road, where band concerts and fireworks displays were held. The other municipal parks, which at least began to be developed by the early twentieth century, were, like Dunville Park, gifts to the city. The land for Musgrave Park at Balmoral was donated by Henry Musgrave in 1920, the park opening in 1924; Glenbank Park at Ligoniel, the gift of G. Herbert Ewart, also given in 1920, opened in 1923.[212]

NOTES

1 John Dubourdieu, *A statistical survey of the County of Antrim, with observations on the means of improvement* (Dublin, 1812); Stephen A. Royle, *Belfast, part II, 1840 to 1900: Irish historic towns atlas no. 17* (Dublin, 2007).
2 Anthony C. Hepburn and Brenda Collins, 'Industrial society: the structure of Belfast, 1901' in Peter Roebuck (ed.) *Plantation to partition: essays in Ulster history in honour of J.L. McCracken* (Belfast, 1981), pp. 210–28.
3 *BNL*, 20 August 1813, 28 January 1825.
4 Ibid., 26 May 1757.
5 Ibid., 26 September 1758.
6 George Benn, *The history of the town of Belfast* (Belfast, 1823), p. 86.
7 *BNL*, 3 July 1827.
8 BCM, 2 September 1844 (PRONI, LA/7/2/EA/1).
9 BCM, 1 July 1847 (PRONI, LA/7/2/EA/2).
10 O'Neill, 'Sanitary science', p. 42.
11 *BNL*, 27 March 1804, 30 March 1804.
12 BCM, 1 August 1845 (PRONI, LA/7/2/EA/1).
13 *Belfast municipal boundaries: copy of Captain [Francis Y.] Gilbert's report upon the proposed extension of the boundaries of the borough of Belfast; together with copies of all documents laid before him, approving or objecting to such extension*, H.C. 1852–3 (958), xciv, p. 2 and Appendix K (no. 6).
14 Ibid., p. 3.
15 Ibid., pp. 3–4.

16 BCM, 9 December 1896 (PRONI, LA/7/2/EA/20).
17 'Belfast Corporation Bill (by Order)', H.C. debate, 6 March 1896, xxxviii, cc. 310–17 (http://hansard.millbanksystems.com/commons/1896/mar/06/belfast-corporation-bill-by-order) (25 August 2011).
18 Ibid.
19 *BNL*, 17 July 1739.
20 Ibid., 19 January 1779.
21 Ibid., 15 January 1799.
22 Raymond Gillespie, *Early Belfast: the origins and growth of an Ulster town to 1750* (Belfast, 2007).
23 *BNL*, 6 August 1765.
24 Ibid., 27 August 1765.
25 W.A. Maguire, *Living like a lord: the second marquis of Donegall, 1769–1844* (Belfast, 1984).
26 Ibid., pp. 9, 12.
27 Ibid., p. 25.
28 *BNL*, 11 December 1829.
29 William Murphy O'Hanlon, *Walks among the poor of Belfast and suggestions for their improvement* (Belfast, 1853) (reprinted Wakefield, 1971), p. 101.
30 R.M. Young, 'Old times in Belfast' in *Journal of the Royal Society of Antiquaries of Ireland*, xxxv, no. 4 (1905), p. 381.
31 *BNL*, 11 October 1844.
32 W.A. Maguire, 'Lord Donegall and the sale of Belfast: a case history from the Encumbered Estates Court' in *Economic History Review*, xxix, no. 4 (1976), pp. 570–84.
33 Maguire, *Living like a lord*, p. 95.
34 Maguire, 'Lord Donegall', pp. 582, 583.
35 *BNL*, 19 December 1780.
36 Benn, *History of the town of Belfast*, p. 85.
37 Belfast 1837 valuation field books (PRONI, VAL/1/B/74A). See also Stephen A. Royle, 'The socio-spatial structure of Belfast in 1837: evidence from the First Valuation' in *Irish Geography*, xxiv, no. 1 (1991), pp. 1–9.
38 *Belfast municipal boundaries*, p. 5.
39 R. Timothy Campbell and Stephen A. Royle, 'East Belfast and the suburbanization of north-west County Down in the nineteenth century' in L.J. Proudfoot (ed.), *Down, history and society: interdisciplinary essays on the history of an Irish county* (Dublin, 1997), pp. 629–62.
40 *BNL*, 9 December 1760.
41 Raymond Gillespie and Stephen A. Royle, *Belfast, part I, to 1840: Irish historic towns atlas no. 12* (Dublin, 2003).
42 Alison Jordan, *Who cared? Charity in Victorian and Edwardian Belfast* (Belfast, 1993), pp. 12, 15; *Third report of commissioners for inquiring into the condition of the poorer classes in Ireland* [43] H.C. & H.L. 1836, xxx, p. 38. See also Niall Ó Ciosáin, 'The Poor Inquiry and Irish society' in *Transactions of the Royal Historical Society*, xx (2010), pp. 127–39.
43 O'Hanlon, *Walks among the poor*, p. 1.
44 BCM, 1 May 1849, 1 June 1849, 2 July 1849, 1 August 1849 (PRONI, LA/7/2/EA/2).
45 *BNL*, 5 June 1840.
46 O'Hanlon, *Walks among the poor*, p. 28.
47 Ibid., p. 31.

48 Ibid., p. 59.
49 Ibid., p. 15.
50 Ibid., p. 76.
51 BCM, 1 March 1871 (PRONI, LA/7/2/EA/9).
52 O'Neill, 'Sanitary science', p. 39.
53 Ibid., p. 42.
54 Ibid.
55 Emrys Jones, 'The social geography of Belfast' in *Journal of the Statistical and Social Inquiry Society of Ireland*, xxix, no. 2 (1954), p. 4.
56 Jordan, *Who cared?*
57 Department of the Environment for Northern Ireland, *McMaster Street Conservation Area* (Belfast, 1994).
58 BCM, 21 December 1864 (PRONI, LA/7/2/EA/7).
59 BCM, 1 July 1865 (PRONI, LA/7/2/EA/7); 'And to be judicially noticed', H.C. debate, 6 July 1865, clxxx, c. 1184 (http://hansard.millbanksystems.com/commons/1865/jul/06/and-to-be-judicially-noticed#S3V0180P0_18650706_HOC_329) (25 August 2011).
60 BCM, 1 August 1879 (PRONI, LA/7/2/EA/13).
61 *BNL*, 7 November 1758.
62 Ibid., 5 June 1764.
63 Ibid., 2 October 1764.
64 Ibid., 29 December 1776.
65 Ibid., 20 March 1778.
66 Ibid., 11 October 1782.
67 Ibid., 19 November 1782.
68 Ibid., 4 October 1791.
69 Ibid., 14 August 1798.
70 Benn, *History of the town of Belfast*, p. 88.
71 The Belfast Police Act, 1800: an act for paving, cleansing, and lighting, and improving the several streets, squares, lanes and passages within the town of Belfast (40 & 41 Geo. III, c. 37 [Ire.]) (extracts printed in Book: problems of a growing city: Belfast, 1973 (PRONI, ENV/17/11/4A, ENV/17/11/4B)).
72 *BNL*, 2 October 1801, 14 February 1802.
73 Ibid., 20 September 1812.
74 Ibid., 7 June, 1816.
75 Ibid., 15 February 1820.
76 Ibid., 21 April 1820.
77 Ibid., 24 June 1823.
78 Ibid., 11 June 1822.
79 Ibid., 14 January 1823.
80 Ibid., 4 March 1828.
81 Ibid., 7 March 1820.
82 Ibid., 19 November 1782.
83 Ibid., 29 November 1793.
84 Ibid., 7 August 1795.
85 Ibid., 13 October 1772.
86 Ibid., 19 November 1784.
87 Ibid., 1 November 1814.
88 Ibid., 12 November 1817.
89 O'Hanlon, *Walks among the poor*, p. 27.

90 Andrew G. Malcolm, *The sanitary state of Belfast with suggestions for its improvement* (Belfast, 1852), pp. 7, 8.
91 Ibid., p. 8.
92 O'Neill, 'Sanitary science'.
93 Jack Loudan, *In search of water, being a history of the Belfast water supply* (Belfast, 1940).
94 *BNL*, 9 May 1755.
95 Ibid., 26 October 1762.
96 Malcolm, *Sanitary state*, p. 6.
97 Ibid., p. 7.
98 *BNL*, 18 July 1825.
99 Loudan, *In search of water*, p. 18.
100 *BNL*, 2 July 1784.
101 Belfast Police Act, 1800.
102 *BNL*, 20 March 1795.
103 Ibid., 13 December 1791.
104 Ibid., 16 February 1790.
105 Ibid., 20 July 1795.
106 Ibid., 28 August 1801, 9 September 1802.
107 Ibid., 19 June 1810.
108 Benn, *History of the town of Belfast*; *BNL*, 4 October 1825.
109 Ibid., 14 April 1837.
110 Ibid., 20 March 1840.
111 Ibid., 12 April 1839.
112 Ibid., 25 March 1842.
113 Ibid., 22 August 1842
114 Malcolm, *Sanitary state*, p. 7.
115 John F. Bateman, Report on the supply of water to the town of Belfast, 1855 (LHL, N3283).
116 Loudan, *In search of water*.
117 O'Hanlon, *Walks among the poor*, p. 32.
118 Ibid.
119 Des O'Reilly, *Rivers of Belfast: a history* (Newtownards, 2010).
120 *BNL*, 10 November 1772.
121 Benn, *History of the town of Belfast*; *BNL*, 28 October 1814, 21 February 1815.
122 *BNL*, 20 September 1812.
123 Ibid., 28 May 1819.
124 Ibid., 2 April 1822.
125 Ibid., 12, April 1822, 19 April 1822, 26 April 1822.
126 Ibid., 12 February 1830.
127 Ibid., 11 March 1836.
128 Ibid., 19 July 1836.
129 Ibid., 2 March 1838.
130 Ibid., 3 April 1840.
131 Ibid., 16 June 1840.
132 BCM, 1 August 1844 (PRONI, LA/7/2/EA/1).
133 BCM, 1 October 1886 (PRONI, LA/7/2/EA/1).
134 *Irish Builder*, 15 September 1890.
135 D.J. Owen, *A short history of the port of Belfast* (Belfast, 1917).
136 *BNL*, 4 November 1791.
137 Ibid., 25 August 1769.

138 Ibid., 1 February 1785.
139 Robin Sweetnam and Cecil Nimmons, *Port of Belfast, 1785–1985: an historical review* (Belfast, 1985).
140 Owen, *Port of Belfast*.
141 *BNL*, 23 November 1832.
142 Sweetnam and Nimmons, *Port of Belfast*.
143 O'Hanlon, *Walks among the poor*, p. 67.
144 BCM, 1 June 1871 (PRONI, LA/7/2/EA/9).
145 BCM, 1 March 1872 (PRONI, LA/7/2/EA/10).
146 BCM, 2 July 1877 (PRONI, LA/7/2/EA/12).
147 BCM, 1 November 1884 (PRONI, LA/7/2/EA/15).
148 Material regarding the history of tramways, 1877–1970 (PRONI, LA/7/26/M/1).
149 *BNL*, 28 January 1825.
150 Ibid., 13 January 1837.
151 Ibid., 30 August 1839.
152 Ibid., 1 January 1837.
153 Ibid., 28 February 1845
154 Ibid., 6 September 1844.
155 Jonathan Bardon, *Belfast: an illustrated history* (Belfast, 1982).
156 Wm Bald, FRS, Civil Engineer to [Board of Works, Dublin?], May 1834 (PRONI, Wallace papers, T1009/268, pp. 9–17).
157 *BNL*, 11 September 1840.
158 BCM, 1 December 1863 (PRONI, LA/7/2/EA/7).
159 Ibid., 1 September 1865.
160 BCM, 1 November 1869 (PRONI, LA/7/2/EA/9).
161 Annual report of the LMA, 1892 (PRONI, D2088/11/2).
162 Ibid., 1898 and 1899.
163 *BNL*, 30 December 1757.
164 Ibid., 4 September 1761.
165 Ibid., 14 September 1762.
166 Ibid., 2 October 1764.
167 Ibid., 19 October 1773.
168 Ibid., 10 July 1810.
169 Ibid., 4 September 1798.
170 Ibid., 22 August 1817.
171 Ibid., 7 December 1821.
172 PRONI, Belfast Corporation Gas Works papers, D2177/1.
173 *BNL*, 1 September 1823.
174 Ibid., 9 September 1823.
175 Proposals of the proprietors of the Belfast Gas Works after the transfer of the contract from the Commissioners of Police to the company, 1826 (PRONI, Belfast Corporation Gas Works papers, D2177/1).
176 BCM, 1 January 1857 (PRONI, LA/7/2/EA/5); *Belfast Evening Telegraph*, 14 November 1893.
177 BCM, 21 February 1865 (PRONI, LA/7/2/EA/7).
178 BCM, 2 December 1872 (PRONI, LA/7/2/EA/10).
179 BCM, 21 July 1874 (PRONI, LA/7/2/EA/11).
180 BCM, 1 December 1878 (PRONI, LA/7/2/EA/13).
181 BCM, 1 February 1894 (PRONI, LA/7/2/EA/1), 1 June 1894 (PRONI, LA/7/2/EA/20), 1 January 1895 (PRONI, LA/7/2/EA/21).
182 BCM, 1 July 1896 (PRONI, LA/7/2/EA/20).

183 *Irish Builder*, 12 October 1898.
184 Belfast Police Act, 1800.
185 *BNL*, 3 March 1797.
186 Ibid., 8 August 1800.
187 Ibid., 26 May 1818.
188 Malcolm, *Sanitary state*, p. 9.
189 *BNL*, 27 April 1824.
190 Ibid., 15 June 1827.
191 Eamon Phoenix, *Two acres of Irish history: a study through time of Friar's Bush and Belfast, 1570–1918* (Belfast, 2001).
192 BCM, 14 October 1863 (PRONI, LA/7/2/EA/6).
193 *BNL*, 16 July 1847.
194 BCM, 14 December 1865 (PRONI, LA/7/2/EA/7).
195 Tom Hartley, *Written in stone: the history of Belfast City Cemetery* (Belfast, 2006).
196 Robert Scott, *A breath of fresh air: the story of Belfast's parks* (Belfast, 2000).
197 Malcolm, *Sanitary state*, p. 6.
198 Scott, *A breath of fresh air*.
199 Owen, *Port of Belfast*.
200 Scott, *A breath of fresh air*.
201 Ibid.
202 *BNL*, 19 May 1840.
203 Ibid., 2 June 1840.
204 James Thomson, *On public parks in connexion with large towns, with a suggestion for the formation of a park in Belfast* (Belfast, 1852).
205 O'Hanlon, *Walks among the poor*, p. 84.
206 Ibid.
207 Scott, *A breath of fresh air*.
208 BCM, 17 November 1886 (PRONI, LA/7/2/EA/16).
209 BCM, 1 December 1893 (PRONI, LA/7/2/EA/19).
210 Scott, *A breath of fresh air*.
211 BCM, 1 January 1895 (PRONI, LA/7/2/EA/19).
212 Scott, *A breath of fresh air*.

2

'A PERMANENT AND PROFITABLE CHANNEL OF INDUSTRIAL ENTERPRISE'

During the period covered in this book a transition in industrial production techniques and marketing occurred – from manufacture for local demand to manufacture for regional, national and even international demand. Regarding England, Philip Waller has written:

> The local provision of services including manufactures was encroached upon in the second half of the nineteenth century. Especially significant was the way in which the traditional country town became little more than the agent for city or big firm interests as long-standing local industries collapsed in the face of competition from major capitalist concerns.[1]

Earlier, Waller stated that some English towns 'demonstrated an imperial tendency' to annex the trade of others.[2] On the adjoining island, Belfast became another 'imperial' city and was certainly the site of 'major capitalist concerns'. It was not inevitable that this would happen. With the benefit of hindsight, however, one can recognise early signs of the development of Belfast's industrial might in the eighteenth century, even when there remained many manufacturers and firms who were traditional local producers. One would have been David Watson, a coppersmith, who in 1758 opened a shop near the Market House where he manufactured 'brewing pans, stills, boilers, saucepans, tea kettles and coffee pots'.[3] However, that same year Belfast's growing industrial reach was seen in an announcement that:

> Thomas Lyle, James McWatters and Co of Belfast have begun the rope-making business, and intend carrying it on in a more extensive

manner than hitherto done in this town, on the walk formerly occupied by William McFadden ... They design selling ... all kind of ship's rigging and white work.[4]

Exports became a focus for the town's business community; thus in a letter of 1765 a merchant wrote to his son about the best place for a merchants' exchange, bridges and other infrastructure needed to ease the operation of the docks, a place suited for a shipyard, another for 'public slaughter houses to prepare and salt beef for foreign markets, likewise a fitt place for the timber yards rather than where they are at present'.[5] An example of early large-scale industrial development can be found in a 1774 report:

> in these last few days Stewart Hadskis cast at his foundry in Belfast ... an iron bleaching furnace, which contains upwards of 700 gallons, and is believed to be the largest furnace ever cast in this kingdom[.][6]

This firm also made pots and griddles and other domestic items which found a local market.[7] The 'imperial' industries were mostly associated with developments in the nineteenth and early twentieth centuries, especially regarding shipbuilding and linen.

'She is the largest vessel ever built in this port': shipbuilding

Belfast shipbuilding is associated in the popular imagination with the Victorian foundation of Harland and Wolff, but its history is longer and more complex, stretching back into the seventeenth century, with a revival from the late eighteenth century. Thus in 1810 the *Belfast News Letter* announced the launch of 'a beautiful ship named the *James*, upwards of 400 tons ... from Mr William Ritchie's ship-yard'. The *James* was 'the largest vessel ever built in this port, is calculated to mount 18 guns, and is intended for the West India trade'.[8] Another was the *George*, 300 tons, launched the following year, built entirely of Irish oak and destined for the London trade.[9]

Ritchie was a Scottish shipbuilder who had set up in Belfast in 1791 at the inducement of local merchants and the Ballast Board, which provided him with space at Lime Kiln Dock, on the County Antrim side of the Lagan. His first vessel, fittingly called the *Hibernian*, had been launched in 1792. William Ritchie founded a dynasty as well as a firm. His brother and partner, Hugh, opened his own shipyard in 1798, which in 1807 passed to another brother, John, who had been building ships in Scotland. John Ritchie then went into partnership with Alexander McLaine, who married Ritchie's daughter. On John Ritchie's death the enterprise became Alexander McLaine and Sons.[10] In 1815 William Ritchie took on a nephew as a partner,[11] and five years later announced that he intended to quit business and would let or sell his shipbuilding yard.[12] Charles Connell took on its management, buying the yard in 1824. In 1838 Kirwan and McCune (later recast as Thompson and Kirwan) commenced shipbuilding at Dunbar's Dock.

The first Irish-built steam vessel, the *Belfast*, was launched by Ritchie and McLaine in 1820 for Belfast man George Langtry. In July Langtry sailed the *Belfast* to Liverpool with many passengers aboard; 'a vast crowd of spectators lined the quays and gave three cheers when she set off'.[13] The engines had been supplied by the Lagan Foundry of Coates and Young, who in 1838 had built the first local iron ship, the *Countess of Caledon*, to tow lighters on Lough Neagh.[14] The shipbuilding industry was certainly active; in a single issue in 1841 the *Belfast News Letter* mentioned: a brig of 206 tons launched from Thompson and Kirwan; a vessel with a raised quarterdeck from Connells' yard; a brig and a pleasure yacht from Alexander McLaine's yard; and a schooner from McCune, now based in Ballymacarrett.[15] In 1845 the Ballast Board purchased all private docks and quays. This adversely affected the shipyards on the County Antrim bank and, in a somewhat reluctant gesture of compensation, the board agreed to provide a patent slip on Dargan's Island and also a small shipyard next to it, which Thompson and Kirwan took. (A patent slip is a piece of ground sloping into the water up and down which ships can be winched on cradles; it is cheaper to construct, if less convenient to use, than a dry (graving) dock.) Coates and Young just rented facilities when needed, whilst another slip was built for the McLaine and Connell yards on the Antrim shore. However, Connell soon left shipbuilding for the more lucrative business of ship repair.[16]

The future of Belfast shipbuilding was certainly not secure at this time, but in 1847 the *Belfast News Letter* presciently announced that iron shipbuilding in Belfast was likely to become 'a permanent and profitable channel of industrial enterprise', and a large number of workmen might expect to be employed. The basis of this forecast was the fact that Coates and Young were building an iron steamer of the substantial size of 600 tons.[17] In 1853, after a long deliberation, the Harbour Commissioners facilitated the development of iron shipbuilding by providing a new 1-acre (0.4-hectare) shipyard on Queen's Island for Edward Hickson of the Eliza Foundry, which had opened in 1851. This was located on the opposite side of the patent slip to Thompson and Kirwan, and Hickson had permission to use the steam-engine winch at the slip. Hickson soon constructed a second berth and began to launch ships in 1854. One Edward Harland, a Yorkshireman aged twenty-three, was employed as the yard's second manager in December 1854.

Harland had been an apprentice at Robert Stephenson's engineering works on the Tyne and had worked on the Clyde before returning to Newcastle as manager for Thomas Toward's yard. Hickson quickly lost his Eliza Street business, which affected the shipyard. Another problem for Harland was that the first manager of Hickson's shipyard, who had been dismissed, took over the former premises of Thompson and Kirwan on the County Antrim shore in competition. However, Harland was able to recruit people from the Newcastle yard where he had worked and began to launch ships. In 1857 Harland employed as his assistant Gustav Wolff, nephew of his friend Gustav Schwabe, the Liverpool shipowner. In 1858, having failed to get permission to open yards in Liverpool, Harland accepted Hickson's invitation to buy the yard in Belfast. He increased its capacity and potential by also taking the Thompson and Kirwan business on the other side of the slip, giving the enterprise a total working area of 3.5 acres (1.4 hectares). Orders came from the Bibby Line in Liverpool, in which Schwabe was a partner. At first called Edward James Harland and Company, when Harland made Gustav Wolff his partner in 1861 the firm became Harland and Wolff.[18]

As Jonathan Bardon puts it:

> in some respects the rapid emergence of Belfast as a shipbuilding
> centre was accidental: a debt-laden ironworks just happened to
> engage one of the greatest engineering geniuses of the day.[19]

Moreover, although Belfast and its region could provide no raw
materials for shipbuilding, there was a ready availability of easily
worked reclaimed land for shipyards. At any rate, given the expansion
of global trade in the Victorian period, the time was ripe for
shipbuilding to prosper. Of no less importance for Harland and Wolff,
which specialised in passenger ships, was the increase in mass
migration, especially from Europe to North America. Many migrants
were transported in Harland's innovative 'coffin' ships, so called
because of their long, slim shape, by companies such as the White Star
Line (bought by the Oceanic Steam Navigation Company), which had
many vessels built on Queen's Island. By 1863 the Harbour
Commissioners were in a position to provide a large tidal basin and
graving dock on the island. This had been planned earlier but had been
delayed by the downturn in the economy after the Crimean War and
a dispute about which side of the river it should be situated on. The
Abercorn Basin and Hamilton Graving Dock finally opened in 1867.

By 1875 Harland and Wolff had grown into a large yard with a
workforce of over a thousand. In that year they reconstructed the firm
to take on three new partners: the yard manager and the head of engine
design, brothers Walter and Alexander Wilson (although the latter
soon withdrew) and the chief draughtsman, the 'hypnotic' William
Pirrie, who became dominant in both the company and shipbuilding
in general well into the twentieth century.[20] In their history of Harland
and Wolff, Moss and Hume wrote that by the mid-1870s:

> The success of the firm was due in large measure to the confidence
> of Gustav Christian Schwabe and his partners John S. Bibby and
> Thomas Ismay [who had ordered many of the ships] in the ability of
> Harland and Wolff to design and construct new, technically
> advanced tonnage, which would prove commercially viable. Harland
> and Wolff had more than justified this faith. They had shown
> themselves to be remarkably effective partners.[21]

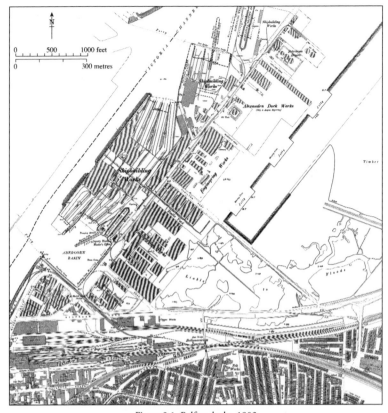

Figure 2.1 Belfast docks, 1902

The later 1870s were a difficult time economically, but in 1878 Harland and Wolff bought out McLaine's shipyard, the history of which stretched back to the days of the Ritchies, and also built an expensive new engine and boiler works. Harland and Wolff acquired the rest of Queen's Island, the park site, between 1877 and 1879 and constructed four building berths there. An upturn in the early 1880s proved the prescience of these investments and, although this was quickly followed by a downturn, matters improved again later in the decade. The huge, 800-foot (244-metre) Alexandra Graving Dock was built on the now much larger Queen's Island between 1885 and 1889. This meant the original patent slip was no longer required (Figure 2.1).

A serious fire in 1896 provided the catalyst for further reorganising the yard.[22] Adding an element of symbolism, this was after the death of

56

Sir Edward Harland in 1895, who was buried in the City Cemetery with great pomp, his cortege led by 500 shipyard workers.[23] Berths were rebuilt; gantries were erected to quicken production; the engine and boiler works were re-equipped. The *Oceanic*, at 17,274 tons the largest ship ever built, was produced using the new facilities in 1899, a period in which Harland and Wolff were turning away orders.[24] The Thompson Graving Dock (Figure 2.2) was completed by 1911, after a difficult building process during which subsidence had put the adjacent Alexander Dock out of commission for several years. Thompson Dock, at 850 feet (259 metres) had as its first tenant, the *Olympic*. Weighing 45,324 tons, it was at that time the world's largest ship.

A new deep-water fitting-out berth at Thompson Wharf East opened in 1917. In that year D.J. Owen's history of the port of Belfast was published; in it he noted that Harland and Wolff by then employed up to 17,000 workers on a 135-acre (55-hectare) site. Owen listed a number of famous ships built by the company including the *Olympic* and the *Britannic*, but the *Titanic* was not mentioned.[25]

At 46,328 tons, the *Titanic* had been the largest ship ever built. The sinking of the *Titanic* on her maiden voyage in 1912 has come to be seen as symbolic of the subsequent industrial and commercial decline of Belfast. However, at the time, the major immediate problem for Harland and Wolff was the death of their chief designer, Thomas Andrews, Lord Pirrie's nephew, who had been on board. In fact, Harland and Wolff won business as a result of the *Titanic*'s loss, refitting ships to improve their safety equipment in the light of the new regulations that were introduced. During World War I Harland and Wolff managed to retain most of their workforce against competition from the forces and accepted naval contracts including a cruiser, HMS *Glorious*, several urgent orders for monitors (naval gun boats) and many orders for 'standard' ships for merchant use. The company also built bombers. After the war there was a period of heavy orders as companies and nations re-equipped before the harder years of the late 1920s and the depression.

Harland and Wolff had wished to extend their facilities in Belfast on land by the Musgrave Channel since this had opened in 1903, but a long dispute saw them having to wait to construct their East Yard until 1919. During this hiatus the company had taken capacity in

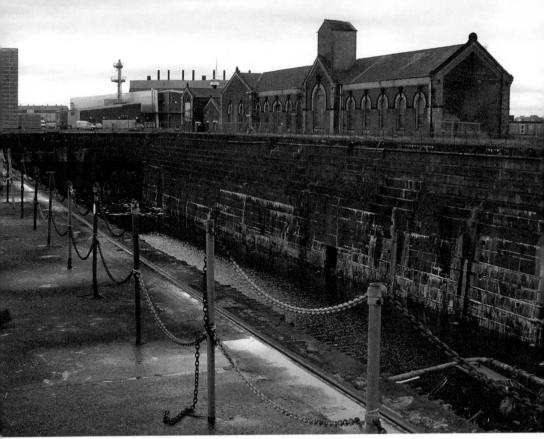

Figure 2.2 Thompson Graving Dock

Southampton and on the Clyde. Having facilities in Great Britain was also a possible refuge for the firm in case there were civil disturbances or unwelcome political developments in Ulster. Plans had been made to relocate if Home Rule were granted, but partition meant that Harland and Wolff remained in Belfast. William Pirrie, who had taken on the position of Controller General of Merchant Shipping during the war, became a viscount and a senator in the new Northern Ireland parliament. He died at seventy-eight in 1924 whilst on a cruise off Chile. His embalmed body was fittingly brought home across the Atlantic on the *Olympic* for burial in Belfast City Cemetery sixty-two years after he had joined Harland and Wolff.[26]

There were other shipyards. MacIlwaine and Lewis (later MacIlwaine and MacColl) of the Ulster Iron Works started to build ships on reclaimed land north of Queen's Island in 1884. Five years earlier, Frank Workman and George Clark, once both apprentices to Harland and Wolff, started to build ships. Their firm, Workman Clark, laid the keel of its first ship in 1880 on a 4-acre (1.6-hectare) site on the County Antrim side of the Lagan. They built two steamers of 400 tons each in the first year, when they employed 150 men. Fifteen years later this, the 'wee yard', employed 14,000 men and launched 34,000 tons of shipping from 14 acres (5.7 hectares) of shipyard, having taken over the MacIlwaine yard in 1893. In 1902 the 'wee yard' was 50 acres (20 hectares) in extent and the 75,800 tons launched comprised the largest output in the world – a rank the yard held also in 1909, when 88,200 tons of shipping were launched. In 1920, on a 100-acre (40-hectare) site, Workman Clark employed 10,000 workers.[27] The firm did not survive the Great Depression, however, closing in 1939.

These shipyards and their workers dominated Belfast – both its skyline and, at certain times of the day, its streets. As Wilfred Ewart wrote in 1922:

> If Belfast's characteristic sound is the clangour of tramcar bells, her characteristic hour is 5.30 p.m. Then the shipyard workers crowd out of the docks until Waring Street and High Street are blocked with them ... In Belfast you have the spectacle of special trams labelled 'Workers only', crowded from roof to floor and passing in procession at this hour down High Street.[28]

'We must look upon the linen trade as our staple industry': Linenopolis

Belfast's mighty textile industry had unlikely and humble beginnings in cotton spinning, once this had spread from its initial origin as a make-work scheme in the Poor House on Clifton Street. Nicolas Grimshaw, who had developed a water-powered carding machine at his home, presented it to the Poor House in 1778, where it was worked by hand. He followed this gift with a spinning machine. In 1779 Robert Joy and Thomas McCabe set up a water-powered cotton-spinning mill near the institution and by February 1780 twenty-three children from the Poor House were employed there. Other small factories were then established. Nicholas Grimshaw himself, along with Nat Wilson, erected one in Whitehouse, outside Belfast, in 1784 and followed it with developments in Lisburn. Shortly afterwards there were more factories in Belfast, perhaps stimulated by the 'curious working models of machinery in the cotton line' that were exhibited in the town 'by two English adventurers'.[29] Water was the predominant power source initially, but it was soon challenged by steam. By 1811 there were fifteen steam engines in Belfast and district,[30] although other sources of energy remained in use in textile production, including human power in a domestic setting, especially for weaving. George Benn wrote in 1823 that 'in many of the streets and populous roads of the suburbs of the town, particularly at Ballymacarrett, the sound of the loom issues almost from every house'.[31] In his manuscript notes Benn further added:

> When cotton spinning was first introduced into Belfast it took a great hold on the fancy of the people and small mills in various parts of the town ... were set up to make cotton yarn[.] There was one in Waring Street in the beginning of the present century worked by a horse, some in the neighbourhood of Smithfield, with the same motive power, even in the kitchens of the houses ... spinning in a very humble way was carried on. Berry Street in 1793, temporarily acquired the name Factory Row – we may fairly presume from this cause. It spread over the country following at a distance in the wake of the great cotton industry of England.[32]

Some cotton factories became quite large. Press reports in 1813 of the 'dreadful fire ... in the great Cotton Factory in the rear of the Poor House' mention that it was 200 feet (61 metres) long, five storeys high and employed 300 people.[33]

Belfast's industrial districts included the areas of the early water-powered mills:

> when cotton and later linen manufacturing was established on steam power, water was still indispensable, and the factories developed on these rivers, stretching westwards towards the plateau. Later still auxiliary industries such as machine-tool making and engineering arose in the same vicinity, consolidating the industrial belt.[34]

The council minute books are full of references to permission being granted for new industrial developments. For example, the volume relating to the period from March 1882 to November 1884 records

Manufacturing category	Number	Manufacturing category	Number
Aerated water	93	Lime kilns	8
Agricultural implements	28	Machines	69
Alabaster and cement	52	Matches	2
Bakeries	17	Mills (corn, flour,	54
Biscuits	4	meal, barley, seed)	
Bleach greens	5	Muslin	210
Bobbins	2	Nails	1
Bottle works and stores	4	Packing cases	1
Brass and iron foundries	24	Paper	35
Brass foundries	130	Print works	2
Breweries	27	Railway workshops	1
Brick and tile works	13	Rectifying distilleries	26
Brickfields	24	Reeds	1
Button blue	4	Ribbons	1
Cards	3	Rope walks	92
Carts	45	Sails	8
Carver's workshop	1	Salt stores	2
Chemicals	50	Salt works	1
Coaches	79	Saw mills	57
Collars and cuffs	3	Shipyards	24
Cooperages	143	Smithies	10
Cotton and linen	139	Soap and tallow	68
Distilleries	34	Spindles	2
Dye works	1	Starch	66
Factory (unspecified)	1	Stone and marble	14
Fancy boxes	2	Straw bonnets	58
Felt and asphalt	10	Sweets	1
Finishing works	1	Tanneries	7
Forges	19	Tobacco	55
Foundries	13	Turners' workshops	1
Furniture	1	Weighing-machine	5
Glass	18	manufactories	
Glue	12	Whitesmiths	62
Hats	78	Wire gauze factory	1
Iron foundries	49	Works	2
Lard boiling	1	Workshops (unspecified)	1
		Total	**2,078**

Notes:
- This table identifies manufactories that operated at some stage between 1840 and 1900. Not all would have been in existence at the same time.
- There is no indication of the size of the workforce in each case.

Source: calculated from Stephen A. Royle, *Belfast, part II, 1840 to 1900: Irish historic towns atlas no. 17* (Dublin, 2007).

Table 2.1. Manufacturing enterprises in Belfast, 1840–1900.

such permissions for two soap works, three forges, a boiler house and engine shed, four unspecified factories, two workshops, an aerated water factory, a match factory, three flour mills, a paint factory, a weaving shed, a carpenter's shop and a linen mill.[35] Benn's 1823 history provides a useful account of the range of Belfast's industries at that time. He mentions in order: cotton (spinning, weaving, printing, bleaching), calico printing, linen (weaving and bleaching), canvas, rope, paper, iron (casting and engine manufacture), glass, salt, vitriol, brewing, soap, candles, hats, leather, a flour mill, starch, logwood, glue, bricks and lime.[36] The sheer size of the manufacturing industries in Belfast can be seen further from inspection of the fascicle of the *Irish historic towns atlas* relating to Belfast between 1840 and 1900, which has 2,078 entries under 'Manufacturing' in seventy different categories (Table 2.1).[37] Many fed into the shipbuilding and textile-export industries. Others were separate, some being important export industries in their own right, such as in the food and drinks sector (particularly aerated water, where Cantrell and Cochrane were significant). Other firms would have been producing for the local market.

Despite this range of activity, Belfast became 'Linenopolis'. The vice-president of the Linen Merchants' Association was able to claim in 1899 that:

> We have not many industries left us in Ireland. We have established our Linen trade by dint of industry and hard work ... We have other industries in our midst, some of which are so vast as to enable us to launch in our harbour the largest vessel in the world [RMS *Oceanic*] – (applause) – [but] we must look upon the linen trade as our staple industry in this province.[38]

Linen production had not always been a Belfast staple. Rather, it had long been an industry of rural Ulster, with country people processing flax that was locally grown, helped by such innovations as the flying shuttle, 'introduced with success among the Moravians at Ballykennedy' in 1778.[39] Belfast's role was principally in trading the finished product. Unbleached cloth was traded especially in the Brown Linen Hall on Donegall Street (opened in 1754 and replaced in the same street in 1773) and bleached cloth was bought and sold in the White Linen Hall in Donegall Square – a building opened in 1784 and described as 'handsome and light with an extremely neat spire'.[40] It was designed by Roger Mulholland, who inserted numerous rooms intended largely as the offices of linen drapers.

Benn noted in 1823 that 'there is very little linen cloth woven in this town or parish', in contrast to bleaching, there being within the parish of Belfast 'twelve bleach greens which beautify the country and give employment to its inhabitants'.[41] *The Times* published helpful statistics: £275,000 worth of linen had been exported from the region in 1782, at which time there were thirty-nine bleach greens within an 8-mile (12.9-kilometre) radius of Belfast with bleaching products worth £430,000 that year; seventeen bleach greens were at work in the same area in 1814, bleaching £646,666 worth of cloth. The linen was exported throughout the British Empire and also to Spanish America.[42]

Then came the shift in the focus of Belfast's factory production from cotton to linen. In 1824 the Mulholland brothers, Thomas and Andrew, announced that they were to sell their cotton mill in Wine Tavern Street and property in Union Street and move to a new cotton mill in York Street.[43] In 1827 they set up an experimental wet-flax-spinning process in a former cotton factory in Francis Street and in June 1828, after their York Street cotton factory burnt down,[44] they took the opportunity to rebuild it for flax spinning using the wet-flax-spinning method. Their partner, John Hind, had gone to Leeds to see the latest techniques in operation there. The necessary machinery was built in the MacAdam brothers' Soho Foundry in Townsend Street.[45] Other manufacturers followed this transfer of fibres and a report from a visitor in October 1832 mentioned that twelve linen mills were in full work, adding, 'Heavens! How pleasing, how delightful is the contrast which Belfast exhibits as compared with the capital of Ireland.'[46] It was not only casual visitors who were impressed. A number of dignitaries were taken round the Ardoyne damask factory in 1833, including Lord John Russell, later to be twice prime minister, who was then paymaster general.[47]

Samuel Lewis, in *The topographical dictionary of Ireland*, usefully summarised the situation up to 1837:

> In 1830 a very extensive mill was erected for spinning linen yarn on the same principle as in the chief houses at Leeds, in order to meet

the increasing demands of the manufacturers; and, in 1832, a large cotton mill was adapted to the spinning of the refuse flax of the linen mill for the use of the canvas weavers. In these two mills more than 700 persons are employed and, since their erection a linen cloth manufactory has been erected on a very large scale at Ligoneil [*sic*] two miles distant, which is the first of its kind in this part of the country. Seven more spinning mills containing 48,000 spindles and affording employment to more than 5,000 persons were erected in 1834, and several others have been erected since and are mostly five stories high.[48]

A contemporary description of the Mulhollands' York Street factory states:

In one factory alone my worthy friend Dr Mulholland has five hundred handsome girls [who] work in huge long chambers lighted by numbers of windows, hot with steam, buzzing and humming with thousands of whirling wheels that all take their motion from a steam engine which lives apart in a cast-iron temple of its own from which it communicates with the innumerable machines that the five hundred girls preside over. They have seemingly but to take away the work when done – the enormous monster in the cast-iron room does it all. He cards the flax, combs it, spins it, beats it and twists it. The five hundred girls stand by to feed him or take the material away from him when he has had his will of it. There is something frightful in the vastness as in the minuteness of his power.[49]

At first most of the new machinery for linen manufacture was imported but Alan McCutcheon has written that by 1852 there were six makers of flax-spinning machinery in Belfast, of which three foundries – Belfast, Albert and Falls – were particularly significant. He stated that the 'Belfast makers came to be regarded as a serious threat to the relative monopoly hitherto enjoyed in this field by engineering firms in Leeds and Manchester'.[50] The Albert Foundry in Albert Street was taken over by its manager, James Mackie, in 1858, who went on to establish Mackie's on the Springfield Road, one of Belfast's most prominent engineering manufactories. Mackie's operated until 1999.

'Once we were prosperous': Luddism and protectionism versus 'the growth of powerful spinning and weaving interests'

The writer of the quotation on the York Street mill above went on to lament the fact that:

> five hundred young women [are] busy at work and earning good wages [but] these 500 girls produce, by the aid of the engine, as much work as five thousand could do without it – thus throwing as it were [more than] four thousand people out of employment.[51]

On a smaller scale in nearby Antrim, Alexander Irvine, recalling his childhood in the 1860s, wrote:

> Once we were prosperous. That was when two older brothers worked with my father at shoemaking. I remember them on winter nights sitting round the big candlestick, one of the three always singing folk songs as he worked. I browsed among the lasts … dreaming of the wonderful days beyond when I, too, could make a boot and sing *Black-eyed Susan*. Then the news came – news of a revolution – 'They're making boots by machinery now'.[52]

Luddite sentiments were unavailing in industrial, capitalist Belfast, even when expressed in most heartfelt terms, as in the 1843 memorial to the prime minister, Sir Robert Peel, from Belfast sawyers. Sawyers had long displayed solidarity – in 1814 there had been a demonstration in which they had assembled in Donegall Street and gone on to search for fellow workmen who, it was thought, had been 'working at prices below which they thought right'.[53] In 1843, the sawyers traced:

> all their sufferings to the following causes, which unproductive of any advantage to the public at large have almost entirely deprived them of the means of earning their daily bread, namely the daily increasing numbers of saw mills, whereby manual labour is almost totally superseded by machinery and the importation from America of large quantities of … planks at a very low rate of duty which are sold here for joists and rafters and various other purposes.[54]

The memorial went on to state that a pair of sawyers could cut 300 superficial feet of timber in a good day's work in twelve hours but a saw mill requiring just six operatives could cut 30,000 feet of timber in the same time, thus doing the work of a hundred pairs. Thus were 194 sawyers thrown out of work and, assuming a family of three, 582 individuals rendered destitute.[55] The *Belfast News Letter* announced the opening of Belfast's first 'patent saw mill' in 1838,[56] and between 1840 and 1900 fifty-seven saw mills operated in Belfast,[57] the manual sawyer, indeed, being 'superseded by machinery'.

To the dismay, doubtless, of the sawyers, the industrialisation of Belfast depended on the two things to which they objected: machine manufacture and international trade. The two subjects had come together in 1824 when the cotton spinners of Belfast had petitioned parliament, asking for the export of cotton-spinning machinery to be forbidden, there being much competition from manufacturers in the USA.[58] This was to no avail – the nineteenth century was increasingly globalised and protectionism, like Luddism, had no place in it. Indeed, Belfast's industries benefited greatly from global markets and international trade, even if shoemakers, sawyers and domestic weavers lost out.

Belfast's district of Ballymacarrett, east of the Lagan, was home to many domestic weavers. They had never been able to live well and in 1830 a charity sermon was preached to raise funds for their relief.[59] In 1842 the Ballymacarrett weavers were in a particularly distressed state: meetings were held to try and raise funds for them,[60] and emigration was arranged. A party of 170 distressed weavers, comprising thirty-four families from Belfast and Ballymacarrett, sailed for Québec in the *Independence* in June.[61] In July, application was made to the Poor Law Commissioners about raising a rate to enable unemployed labourers and weavers 'who are left without the means of support' to emigrate to America.[62] Hand-loom weaving limped along for another generation or so, for in 1891 the Linen Merchants' Association petitioned MPs against a bill about Irish hand-loom weavers passing through parliament. They felt the restrictions it would impose would lead to the speedy demise of what was already a struggling industry.[63]

Like shipbuilding, linen depended upon exports. As the president of the Linen Merchants' Association stated in 1892, 'commerce, instead of being war, is the greatest instrument of peace that the world has ever seen'. A nation that attempted 'to manufacture and produce everything she herself requires, irrespective altogether of conditions of adaption' was 'foolish'.[64] Thus it was to promote trade rather than to express feelings of humanity that in 1902 the Linen Merchants' Association sent a message of condolence to Mrs McKinley and the American people following the assassination of President William McKinley, noting that the USA was the best customer for their wares. There had been a decrease in demand from:

> Those old and valued customers for Irish linens, the West Indies and the South American Republics ... The principal products of those countries were sugar and coffee, and unfortunately the price of those articles was at present so very low as to barely pay the cost of production, and no margin at all was left for the purchase of Irish linen, which in the old times was looked upon by these friends almost more in the light of a necessity than a luxury. It was said that there is at present 800,000 tons of sugar in Cuba for which no market can be found, and to this must be attributed the almost total collapse of this once favourite market for Irish linens. Let them hope that the prosperity which usually follows in the track of freedom might now have some good things in store for this beautiful and fertile land (hear, hear.) In the same way the low price of coffee accounted for the decreased consumption of linen fabrics in many of the West Indian islands, in the Central American Republics, and Brazil, and in Venezuela, and Colombia, and in addition the present disturbed condition of the latter was very much against their interests.[65]

Referring to 1907, when there were severe labour disputes in Belfast, the Linen Merchants' Association noted that those troubles might be said to be 'from within, but, as merchants doing business abroad, they had their own trouble from without in the shape of unreasonable requests from customers and Custom-houses'.[66] That global events affected this industry was seen in the report from the Linen Merchants' Association for 1915. After lamenting the advent of the 'greatest war the world has ever experienced', the report noted that the demand for war materials ensured 'great activity exists in this country [and] the past year for most of us will probably work out a not unprofitable one'.[67]

Industrialisation generally concentrated power and control in the hands of the larger companies. McCutcheon gives the example of linen bleaching:

> As the nineteenth century had progressed so the commercial role of the bleacher in buying, processing and reselling linen had gradually declined with the growth of powerful spinning and weaving interests and by 1900 the commercial sector of the industry was in the hands of the warehouse departments of various large power-loom factories which had emerged during the previous half century, or of linen factors who acted as agents for many of the smaller undertakings.[68]

In 1873, the fifty-two firms that had set up the Linen Merchants' Association at a meeting held (appropriately) in the White Linen Hall had banded together 'owing to some questions of importance having

Mill name	Year closed	Year cleared out	Number of spindles
Browns	1873	1876	5,742
Russell	1873	1876	8,125
Eliza St	1876	1876	6,056
Lawrence	1877	1887	3,428
Buncrana	1877	1890	7,456
Shaw, ED	1878	1878	11,660
Mitchell	1879	1880	16,576
Shaw, Joseph	1879	1880	15,600
Smyth	1882	1882	4,092
Hinds	1883	1887	26,762
Wallis & Pollock	1884	1884	8,000
Moore	1885	1886	900
Morelands	1886	1888	13,000
Belfast	1898	1899	21,400
Ligoniel	1898	1899	11,700
St Mary's	1898	–	10,700
Sprucefield	1901	1901	4,436
Bath Place	1902	–	14,160
Smithfield	1903	1903	10,670
Total			200,463

Source: Typescript list of mills closed in Ireland, *c.* 1904 (PRONI, D2088/22/9).

Table 2.2. Linen mills closed, 1873–1903.

arisen in connexion with the Linen Trade', namely a depression in the industry.[69] Linen had often proved to be fickle. Thus, in 1847, during the famine, there was a depression of trade and the local newspaper reported that four mills with 1,200 operatives had ceased work; another eight were on short time.[70] D.L. Armstrong noted than the Belfast linen industry enjoyed considerable expansion from 1850 to 1861, then boomed as demand rose during the American Civil War, which interrupted supplies of raw cotton from the southern states of the USA. In 1867, after that war had ended and cotton supplies were restored, there was a severe slump.[71] Belfast linen continued to be troubled by competition from cheaper cotton goods. Table 2.2 lists twenty substantial firms that closed between 1873 and 1903, with over 200,000 spindles lost.

The Linen Merchants' Association considered how best to market their produce internationally, attending, for example, the International Exhibition in Philadelphia in 1876 and the Paris Exhibition of 1879.[72] The association protected standards, as in 1899 when it successfully prosecuted a textile firm that was passing off cheaper cotton and union goods as linen; this matter came up again in 1903, for Belfast linen was of high quality.[73] One ghoulish testimonial comes in Raymond Calvert's 1926 comic poem, 'The ballad of William Bloat'. Bloat was a Belfast man cursed with a harridan of a wife. One day at dawn he cut her throat: 'with a razor gash, he settled her hash'. Then, afraid for the consequences of his crime, he resolved to commit suicide and hanged himself with the bedsheet, solemnly cursing the pope with his last breath (he was from the Shankill Road):

> But the strangest turn to the whole concern,
> Is only just beginning,
> He went to Hell but his wife got well,
> And she's still alive and sinning,
> For the razor blade was German made,
> But the sheet was Belfast linen.[74]

(Nationalist alternative versions have the razor blade as English and the linen as Irish).

Other issues for the Linen Merchants' Association were communications, pressing for improved postal services and technological advances such as telephones, which would assist them all.[75] Another general concern was the impact upon business of various factory and workshop acts dating from 1833, set up to ameliorate poor working and welfare conditions. In 1847 a ten-hour working day (excluding breaks) was imposed. In 1874 a fifty-six-hour working week was brought in – five ten-hour weekdays and six hours on Saturday. Armstrong suggests that the attitude of the Irish linen manufacturers to the limitations of hours was, on the whole, unsympathetic.[76] Indeed, in 1876 the Linen Merchants' Association pressed for the 'redress of inequalities and inconsistencies in the various Acts … with the view of suggesting means for equalizing and harmonizing their provisions'.[77] Twenty years later there was bitter comment upon an act 'very hurriedly pushed through the House of Commons' which prohibited employees, especially in the handkerchief trade, from taking work home in the evenings: 'it was not hardship to the girls any more than doing knitting or other light work at home and added materially to their wages'. Indeed, the Linen Merchants' Association considered taking work to do at home after being in the mill all day to be a 'privilege'.[78] In 1902 the Linen Merchants' Association protested about a new factory act that sought to restrict overtime and succeeded in limiting some of its provisions.[79]

'One of the most healthy in the whole range of our manufactures'? Linen industry conditions

Factory acts were seen as necessary by the authorities given the difficult working conditions in the mills. Transforming flax into finished cloth necessitated several distinct processes. First was 'hackling', associated with 'roughing', 'combing' and 'sorting', where the flax was split into fibres. 'Tow', short fibres rejected for high-quality production, was subject to 'carding' to prepare it for spinning. These occupations were usually reserved for boys. In 'preparing' rooms 'spreading' was where women would lay the flax fibres out on belts, which would take ribbons of flax into coils in tall cans for 'drawing' and 'roving' – stretching and twisting the fibres in further preparation for spinning. Flax could be spun wet or dry. The former produced higher-quality cloth and was the method almost universally employed in Belfast. It was necessary to maintain a hot, moist atmosphere for this process. Bobbins full with the spun thread were taken for 'reeling' and 'dressing', whereby the yarn was dried and treated in preparation for being woven into the finished products. Health issues arose from the proximity of the workers to machinery with the potential for accidents as well as from the tiny flax fibres, often called 'pouce', sometimes 'pousse', which would float in the atmosphere especially during hackling and carding, and the heat and dampness of the spinning rooms.

Commentators also began to identify health problems associated with flax working. Friedrich Engels, whilst not mentioning Belfast specifically, wrote that in flax-spinning mills:

> the air is filled with fibrous dust, which produces chest afflictions, especially among workers in the carding and combing-rooms ... Especially unwholesome is the wet spinning of linen-yarn which is carried on by young girls and boys. The water spurts over them from the spindle, so that the front of their clothing is constantly wet through to the skin; and there is always water standing on the floor.[80]

With regard to Belfast itself, one of the most important researchers into occupational health was Dr Andrew Malcolm. Malcolm worked at the General and Fever Hospital, of which he wrote a history,[81] was secretary and registrar of the Lying-in Hospital and lectured at Queen's College Belfast. He also founded the Belfast Society for the Amelioration of the Condition of the Working Classes in 1845 and the Belfast Working Classes' Association for the Promotion of General Improvement the following year.[82] He was secretary of the former and it set up the first public baths and washhouse on Townsend Street in 1847, designed by Charles Lanyon. The society, short of funds, then appealed unsuccessfully for the council to take over the establishment. The council were reluctant and the matter ended up in the Court of Chancery in Dublin, where the ruling was that the council were not obliged to take on the premises. The buildings were eventually sold for a paltry £200 in 1861 and subsequently demolished.[83]

Malcolm's interest in sanitation was further evidenced by his paper to the British Association meeting in Belfast in 1852, where he spoke about Belfast's sewers and drainage, ventilation, water supplies, street cleaning, housing, schools, slaughterhouses and graveyards, all of which had impacts on sanitation and disease. He presented statistical analyses of fevers – Belfast had been afflicted by cholera – and suggested, with the aid of a drawing, improvements for sewerage systems. Forming a small part of this important paper was a section on 'the great working establishments', in which he identified industrial health problems caused by poor ventilation.[84] Malcolm had applied unsuccessfully for the position of what was in effect medical inspector for the spinning factories in 1849, when he was supported by mill owners, and again in 1854, but his biographer was unable to discover if he ever obtained this post before his untimely death in 1856 at the age of thirty-seven.[85] His specific interest in the health of linen-mill workers developed into a major study of their morbidity, which he presented at another British Association meeting at Glasgow in 1855. Here he declared that, Belfast now being a 'factory town', it was the 'duty of all who would wish to see Ireland preserve her powers of competition … to endeavour to remove all impediments to its [linen manufacture's] success'.[86]

Hypothesising that factory employment had 'injurious results', Malcolm first discussed the various processes involved in linen manufacture. Regarding hackling and carding, he was prepared to say that 'a single visit to these departments, in operation, will convince the most sceptical that the functions of the organs of respiration must be materially and injuriously interfered with' by the flax and tow dust. Some processes, particularly spreading, involved continual stooping, which Malcolm found capable of 'interfering injuriously with the vital processes'. By contrast, reeling was least injurious for workers, allowing for a constant change of position and being carried out in normal temperatures. This was unlike the spinning rooms, where temperatures were usually above 90 degrees Fahrenheit (32.2 degrees Celsius). Together with the atmosphere being 'charged with vapour', this left workers constantly perspiring; they were also constantly wet with spray thrown off by the fibres.[87] Although Malcolm did not mention this, problems were also caused by the floors of spinning rooms being wet with polluted water, which affected the workers, especially as many went barefoot.

Malcolm alluded also to the heat being bad for digestion. Two or three times a day spinners would go out into the open air, where contrasting cold, dry conditions led to problems with respiration. He would not accept fatigue as a problem, since hours of work were by then regulated. His text focused upon linen spinning and did not include weaving, but weavers formed part of his subsequent statistical analysis on the morbidity of 2,078 female factory workers, a substantial proportion of the estimated 11,000 factory workers in the town. He also collected statistics on factory workers from the hospitals and dispensaries. Of his sample of female operatives, 73.2 per cent were in good health (defined as 'not complaining'), 10.4 per cent in 'tolerable' health (they 'complained more or less constantly'), leaving 16.2 per cent 'decidedly delicate and requiring medical aid'.[88] He presented details about women who had had to take time away from work (Table 2.3). These and other statistics collected in what was a very extensive study allowed Malcolm to identify that mill workers in Belfast's dispensary districts in all trades and of both genders suffered from gastric ailments, chest diseases and fevers at a rate of more than three per cent above the average. He also found that hacklers had a high rate of chest infections: 'pulmonary disease, generally bronchitis, is *par excellence*, the hackler's malady'.[89] Malcolm's characterisation of the disease as bronchitis is not incorrect, since this word identifies an inflammation. Only in the mid-twentieth century did medical science

Trade	Number in study	Missed work	Incidence rate (%)	Principal causes
Preparers	252	148	58.7	chest, fevers, headache
Spinners	1,281	532	41.5	headache, fevers, stomach/liver
Reelers	457	237	51.9	fevers, chest, stomach/liver
Weavers	78	23	29.5	fevers, headache, debility
Total	*2,068*	*940*	*45.4*	*fevers, headache, chest*

Notes:
- There are no hacklers in the analysis as they were all male.
- The 940 incidents were suffered by 616 individuals, 29.6 per cent of the sample.

Source: adapted from Andrew G. Malcolm, 'The influence of factory life on the health of the operative as founded upon the medical statistics of this class at Belfast' in *Journal of the Statistical Society of London*, xix, no. 2 (1856), pp. 170–81.

Table 2.3. Health statistics, female linen workers, early 1850s.

recognise and name this particular condition as byssinosis, as in Logan's study of flax-dust byssinosis in Belfast, which mentions Malcolm's pioneering work.[90]

Malcolm's conclusion was:

> The marked preponderance of pulmonary infections … evidenced … is a fact of *striking* importance [author's emphasis] … facts … borne out not merely by what we should expect from the nature of the employment, but also from actual experience.[91]

He went on to suggest ways of improving working conditions. These included better ventilation, artificial respirators for hacklers and carders (he regretted that as they were merely boys they could not grow long moustaches to filter air drawn through the mouth) and special mill clothes for spinners, which would be waterproof and worn only at work, allowing them to go out in dry clothes. He was also in favour of mill workers being encouraged to take interest in music and reading to improve their life and encourage them to 'give freely and fully a good day's work for a fair day's wages'. Malcolm concluded with a reminder to mill owners that they must remember that they had duties as well as rights in their 'responsible position as employers'.[92]

Not all Belfast doctors seem to have accepted Andrew Malcolm's assessment, for all its scale and statistical detail. John Moore, a doctor who had mill workers amongst his patients, said at another conference in 1867:

> without exposure to the influence of any noxious gases or emanations, without any unnatural or constrained positions, and without excessive muscular exertion, the employment [of flax spinning] will be found if not one of the most lucrative, at least one of the most healthy in the whole range of our manufactures.[93]

He did accept that roughing was associated with dust and fine particles that 'load the air' and, though they were 'comparatively harmless', he recommended that these impurities should be carried away from operatives by a current of air. Whilst there were 'too often' injuries in hackling, especially mutilation of the fingers and hands of young lads, 'this results, no doubt to a great extent from the fact that boys will be boys'. He recorded that in the preparation room the toil was 'light' and there was no disease 'which arises specifically from or can be traced to the nature of the occupation'. Carding, he accepted, was dangerous, with accidents there often being fatal, but there was comfort in that 'fewer hands are employed in it' than in other departments. Spinning did present problems from the heat and damp and Moore feared for young girls, remarking especially upon trouble with their feet caused by standing all day, barefoot usually, on wet floors.[94]

However, on the whole, Moore found no reason why flax workers should not be remarkably healthy and he ascribed their high rates of sickness to 'other reasons than the nature of the occupation in which they are engaged', namely a poor diet. He was particularly exercised by the reheated tea the mill workers drank, and advised that 'a cooking depôt', presumably a canteen, be provided.[95] It is hard not to see Moore as complacent, if not irresponsible. Conditions did improve somewhat during the later nineteenth century as better equipment was developed and mill workers more often wore shoes, but only in 1906 was it made compulsory to extract dust from the atmosphere and to ensure that the floors were drained.[96]

A contemporary document exists detailing a time series of wages paid to linen spinners from 1866 to 1881 (Table 2.4), which shows that the largely female workforce did not become rich from their long hours spent in unhealthy conditions. Bardon remarked that wages in Belfast flax mills were 'lower than in any other factory-based textile industry in the UK'.[97] Furthermore, modern expectations of annual pay rises were not seen. In fact, the lowest daily rate of 1s 3½d was paid at the end of the period and the highest rate, which was only 1s 6d, was available for just three months in early 1868. The table also reveals that a full week's work, six days, was not always offered by employers and quite often short-time working down to only four days per week was available. This, of course, had an impact on the spinners' take-home pay, which was reduced to 5s 6d per week at its lowest. Others were paid less.

William Topping worked in the linen industry from 1903 to 1956 – at the massive York Street Mill until 1941, when it was damaged in an air raid. He started work at thirteen as a clerk in the telephone office, responsible also for maintaining ledgers and collecting the mailbags twice daily from the ferry from England. This last task was carried out at the start and end of his working day; he had to leave home at 8.15 a.m. to walk to the dock and returned home at 7.00 p.m. In his memoirs he calculated his working week at 56.5 hours, for which he earned four shillings. When he was fourteen he moved into the area of manufacturing, serving his apprenticeship as a damask-loom overlooker, starting work at 6.30 a.m., though for an increased wage of six shillings per week. This went up to eight shillings when he was deemed to be qualified.[98] Topping was obviously aware that he and his workmates laboured in poor conditions. He becomes particularly exercised about one area of the York Street factory called the 'Black Hole'. This room had no natural light or ventilation; in it four looms lit by gas jets were supervised by barefoot children wearing a minimum of clothing. They could work there only on alternate days, such were the conditions. The Black Hole was later converted into a cloakroom, to Topping's satisfaction.

However, Topping conveys the impression that the conditions were generally accepted by the workers. In his weaving shed:

> one can but guess the heat generated by about 500 jets of open gas each evening along with the moist heat required for weaving purposes. This was accepted, with other hardships, as an unavoidable way of life, with no redress.[99]

He does complain about welfare, recounting an incident where he was accidentally struck on the head by a piece of machinery. The foreman washed his wound, applied Friars Balsam to it and added a piece of plaster. Topping, who was permanently scarred, returned to work with 'only 30 minutes lost ... I recorded this incident to show how little interest was taken in the workers' welfare. There was no first aid.'[100]

There were, of course, reactions against what were seen as overweening employers. The Linen Merchants' Association held a special meeting of its council in 1891 to consider a circular from the Irish Linen Lappers' trade union demanding thirty shillings per week for forty-eight hours' work, pondering whether this was an appropriate matter for the association, which had not been formed as an employers' union. Nonetheless, when the linen lappers did strike, it was 'deemed necessary to call upon the members of this association to give notice of dismissal to all union men in their employment'. Seventeen members carried out this policy; three refused and twelve had no union members in their employment. The Linen Merchants' Association

Date	Working week	Wages	Daily rate
January 1866	6 days	8s 9d	1s 5.5d
September 1867	4 days	6s 0d	1s 6d
October 1867	4 days	5s 9d	1s 5.25d
December 1867	4 days	6s 0d	1s 6d
February 1868	6 days	8s 0d	1s 4d
October 1869	4 days	5s 6d	1s 4.5d
December 1869	4.5 days	6s 1.5d	1s 4.33d
January 1870	6 days	8s 0d	1s 4d
April 1870	5.5 days	7s 4.5d	1s 4.09d
April 1870	6 days	8s 0d	1s 4d
September 1871	6 days	8s 6d	1s 5d
April 1872	6 days	9s 0d	1s 6d
December 1873	5 days	7s 7d	1s 5.2d
March 1874	6 days	9s 0d	1s 6d
August 1874	5 days	7s 1d	1s 5d
September 1874	6 days	8s 6d	1s 5d
May 1877	5 days	7s 2d	1s 5.2d
June 1877	6 days	8s 6d	1s 5d
December 1877	5 days	7s 2d	1s 5.2d
April 1878	4 days	5s 10d	1s 5.5d
August 1878	6 days	8s 6d	1s 5d
November 1878	4 days	5s 10d	1s 5.5d
December 1878	6 days	7s 9d	1s 3.5d
November 1879	6 days	8s 6d	1s 5d
October 1880	4.5 days	6s 2d	1s 5.4d
April 1881	6 days	7s 9d	1s 3.5d

Notes:
- Full-time working was six days; often only short-time work was available.
- The daily rate calculated above incorporates the weekly bonus of 6d (3d from October to December 1867).
- Between May and August 1878 alternate weeks of 4 days and 5.75 days were worked.

Source: adapted from Rates of spinners' wages, 1866–81 (PRONI, D2088/27/5).

Table 2.4. Spinners' wages, January 1869–April 1881.

Figure 2.3 Former Owen O'Cork Mill, Beersbridge Road

subsequently met union representatives and offered to withdraw the lockout if the union withdrew the strike.[101]

'Clanging Belfast'

Looking back from the post-industrial era of the twenty-first century it is hard to conceive just how much manufacturing impacted Belfast during its period of industrial pomp. Lost to living memory now are the sensations: the sights, the sounds and presumably also the smells. The transformed Titanic Quarter on Queen's Island, amongst its residences and leisure facilities, will provide research-and-development floor space but its website has no mention of active manufacturing; it is about heritage and tourism now, not shipbuilding. Harland and Wolff still exists but has retreated to cluster around the 1960s building dock at the end of the Musgrave Channel, having given up its earlier spaces on Queen's Island. It no longer builds ships and one can purchase *Titanic* t-shirts from its website. Other than the occasional converted mill, such as the 1911 Owen O'Cork building on Beersbridge Road (Figure 2.3), there are few old industrial buildings actually left standing, let alone carrying out their original function. What we have left are the numbers. Let just one extract from an analysis of the 1901 census convey the significance of industry to what the authors also call 'clanging Belfast':

> by 1901 a minimum of 46 percent of the city's adult male population was engaged in the engineering, shipbuilding, linen, or textile finishing sectors [and] 43 percent of women and girls over the age of ten were at work ... over three fifths of them ... in textile mills or factories, or in the finishing trades.[102]

NOTES

1   Phillip J. Waller, *Town, city and nation: England 1850–1914* (Oxford, 1983), p. 283.
2   Ibid., p. 281.
3   *BNL*, 1 August 1758.
4   Ibid., 13 October 1758.
5   John Black to George Black, 18 July 1765 (PRONI, D1401/5).
6   *BNL*, 27 January 1775.
7   Ibid., 30 December 1777.
8   Ibid., 19 October 1810.
9   Ibid., 22 November 1811.
10 Michael Moss and John R. Hume, *Shipbuilders to the world: 125 years of Harland and Wolff, Belfast 1861–1986* (Belfast, 1986).
11 *BNL*, 10 March 1815, 14 March 1815.
12 Ibid., 15 December 1820.
13 Ibid., 10 March 1815, 14 March 1815, 14 March 1820, 4 July 1820.
14 Ibid., 11 December 1838.
15 Ibid., 4 June 1841.
16 Moss and Hume, *Shipbuilders to the world*.
17 *BNL*, 9 April 1847.
18 Moss and Hume, *Shipbuilders to the world*.
19 Jonathan Bardon, 'Belfast at its zenith' in *History Ireland*, i, no. 4 (winter 1993), p. 50.
20 Moss and Hume, *Shipbuilders to the world*, p. 144.

21 Ibid., p. 35.
22 *BNL*, 27 July 1896.
23 Ibid., 28 December 1895.
24 Moss and Hume, *Shipbuilders to the world.*
25 Owen, *Port of Belfast.*
26 Moss and Hume, *Shipbuilders to the world.*
27 Workman Clark Ltd, shipbuilders and engineers, 1880–1933 (PRONI, D2015/2/2).
28 Wilfrid H.G. Ewart, *A journey in Ireland* (London, 1922), p. 155.
29 *BNL*, 30 November 1787.
30 John J. Monaghan, 'The rise and fall of the Belfast cotton industry' in *Irish Historical Studies*, iii, no. 9 (1942), pp. 1–17.
31 Benn, *History of the town of Belfast*, p. 101.
32 Miscellaneous notes for Benn's history of Belfast, *c.* 1870–7 (PRONI, D3113/4/7).
33 *BNL*, 5 February 1813, 9 February 1813.
34 Jones, 'Social geography', p. 3.
35 BCM, March 1882–November 1884 (PRONI, LA/7/2/EA/15).
36 Benn, *History of the town of Belfast.*
37 Royle, *Belfast part II: Irish historic towns atlas.*
38 Annual report of the LMA, 1899 (PRONI, D2088/11/2).
39 *BNL*, 4 September 1778.
40 Benn, *History of the town of Belfast*, p. 102.
41 Ibid., pp. 102, 103.
42 *The Times*, 7 December 1815.
43 *BNL*, 5 October 1824.
44 Ibid., 1 July 1828.
45 W.A. McCutcheon, *The industrial archaeology of Northern Ireland* (Belfast, 1980).
46 *BNL*, 13 October 1835.
47 Ibid., 11 October 1833.
48 Samuel Lewis, 'Belfast' in *The topographical dictionary of Ireland* (London, 1837), i, p. 194.
49 Notes re the history of Belfast, *c.* 1959 (PRONI, D1239/14).
50 McCutcheon, *Industrial archaeology*, p. 301.
51 Notes re the history of Belfast, *c.* 1959 (PRONI, D1239/14).
52 Alexander Irvine, *My lady of the chimney corner* (New York, 1913), p. 16.
53 *BNL*, 8 July 1814.
54 Memorial of the sawyers of Belfast, 22 May 1843 (BL, Peel papers, ccccxxxiii, Add MS 40613, f. 66b).
55 Ibid.
56 *BNL*, 4 September 1838.
57 Royle, *Belfast part II: Irish historic towns atlas.*
58 *The Times*, 15 April 1824. See also Monaghan, 'Belfast cotton industry'.
59 *BNL*, 12 February 1830.
60 Ibid., 12 April 1842, 19 April 1842, 4 May 1842.
61 Ibid., 3 June 1842.
62 Ibid., 29 July 1842.
63 Annual report of the LMA, 1891 (PRONI, D2088/11/2).
64 Ibid., 1892.
65 Ibid., 1902.
66 Ibid., 1908.

67 Ibid., 1915.
68 McCutcheon, *Industrial archaeology*, p. 312.
69 Annual report of the LMA, 1873 (PRONI, D2088/11/2).
70 *BNL*, 18 May 1847.
71 D.L. Armstrong, 'Social and economic conditions in the Belfast linen industry, 1850–1900' in *Irish Historical Studies*, vii, no. 28 (1951), pp. 235–69.
72 Annual report of the LMA, 1876 (PRONI, D2088/11/2); ibid., 1879.
73 Ibid., 1899; ibid., 1903.
74 Raymond Calvert, 'The ballad of William Bloat' (www.antiromantic.com/ballad-of-william-bloat) (25 August 2011).
75 Annual report of the LMA, 1880 (PRONI, D2088/11/2); ibid., 1881; ibid., 1896; ibid., 1898; ibid., 1899; ibid., 1900.
76 Armstrong, 'Belfast linen industry'.
77 Annual report of the LMA, 1876 (PRONI, D2088/11/2).
78 Ibid., 1896.
79 Ibid., 1902.
80 Friedrich Engels, *The condition of the working class in England* (Leipzig, 1845) (English ed. New York, 1887), p. 447.
81 Andrew G. Malcolm, *The history of the General Hospital, Belfast, and the other medical institutions of the town* (Belfast, 1851) (reprinted in H.G. Calwell, *Andrew Malcolm of Belfast 1818–1856, physician and historian* (Belfast, 1977)).
82 Calwell, *Andrew Malcolm*, Chapter 10.
83 Ibid., Chapter 12.
84 Malcolm, *Sanitary state*.
85 Calwell, *Andrew Malcolm*.
86 Andrew G. Malcolm, 'The influence of factory life on the health of the operative as founded upon the medical statistics of this class at Belfast' in *Journal of the Statistical Society of London*, xix, no. 2 (1856), p. 170.
87 Ibid., p. 173.
88 Ibid., p. 175.
89 Ibid., p. 179.
90 J.S. Logan, 'Flax-dust byssinosis and chronic non-tuberculous chest disease in Belfast', *Ulster Medical Journal*, xxviii, no. 2 (1959), pp. 164–75.
91 Malcolm, 'Influence of factory life', pp. 178–9.
92 Ibid., p. 181.
93 John Moore, 'On the influence of flax spinning on the health of the mill workers of Belfast' in *Transactions of the National Association for the Promotion of Social Science: Belfast meeting 1867* (London, 1868 (also LHL, N13668)).
94 Ibid.
95 Ibid.
96 Armstrong, 'Belfast linen industry'.
97 Bardon, 'Belfast at its zenith', p. 50.
98 William Topping, Memoirs of the working life of William Topping, 1903–1956 (PRONI, D3134/1) (published as *A life in Linenopolis: the memoirs of William Topping, Belfast Damask weaver, 1903–1956* (Belfast, 1992)).
99 Ibid.
100 Ibid.
101 Annual report of the LMA, 1892 (PRONI, D2088/11/1).
102 Hepburn and Collins, 'Industrial society', p. 210.

3

A 'SATURNALIA OF BIGOTRY AND RUFFIANISM': STREET LIFE AND POLITICS

'Overawe the parliament and the government': sedition and repeal

In 1780, the *Belfast News Letter* published three letters from John Allen, a miller, addressed to the 'common people' in the hope that 'the following shrewd thoughts of an illiterate Countryman will be acceptable to that class of readers to whom it is addressed'. The letters, which had been dictated to Allen's local schoolmaster, made a plea for Irish separation from the dominant island to the east: 'Ireland is as free a country as England and has as good a right to be governed by its own laws ... England has no right to make laws for us' read the second letter. The third was even stronger:

> it's truly a hard case that Ireland, which has as good a right to be free
> as any country under the sun, should be so racked and ruined by the
> haughty Englishmen and hindered from making an honest
> livelihood.[1]

The contested political relationships revealed so clearly here by an unlettered miller had much influence on Belfast in the period under discussion in this book.

In 1793 the earl of Westmorland, the lord lieutenant of Ireland, issued a proclamation from Dublin Castle warning against sedition and insurrection and charging 'all persons whomsoever on their allegiance to his majesty to abstain from committing such offences'. There was particular concern about Belfast:

> arms and gunpowder to a very large extent have been sent thither; ...
> bodies of men in arms are drilled and exercised ... the obvious

intention of most of them appears to be to overawe the parliament and the government.[2]

The Belfast authorities were 'to be careful in preserving the peace'; 'seditious and unlawful assemblies' were to be dispersed and offenders dealt with according to the law.[3] Belfast council took the action required, reported *The Times*.[4] Sedition was certainly seen a little later in the 1798 rebellion. Whilst Belfast was not badly affected, unlike Ulster towns such as Saintfield and Antrim, it was involved. Martial law was declared in May, with a curfew being imposed along with a requirement to alert the authorities to any strangers staying in Belfast. Any person 'taken up' by the soldiers after ten o'clock at night was subject to a five-shilling fine.[5] *The Times* reported in June that four brass cannon had been discovered in the town, whilst the turmoil had rendered the services of the Belfast mail coach decidedly unreliable.[6] These were minor incidents and a contemporary historian ascribed Belfast's comparative passivity in 1798 to 'peaceable subjection, by the precaution of the government in placing in it a strong military force'.[7] By August the guards and extra military staff at Belfast were stood down,[8] and a couple of weeks later it was reported that only six people had been executed there, which was considered a small number. *The Times* had moved on to look forward to a good harvest in the area that year.[9] Three years later the Act of Union was marked in Belfast by the hoisting of the Union Flag at the Market House,[10] but the union did not lead to quietude and there were further symptoms of insurrection in 1803, leading to precautions being taken.[11]

Sedition was a nationalist cause, largely supported by Catholics but not exclusively so, given that some of the principals in the 1798 rebellion were Protestant, including Wolfe Tone. In Belfast, one prominent nationalist was William Drennan, a Presbyterian doctor who was one of the founders of the Society of United Irishmen. A petition of 1795 called for 'the entire enfranchisement of the Roman Catholics of this kingdom'.[12] Another, dated 1818, from more than a hundred merchants and gentlemen of Belfast to the town's sovereign, sought to repeal the penal code and so allow Catholics the full advantages of the British constitution.[13] Other petitions to the House of Lords from Ireland, including some from Belfast, were presented to further the cause of Catholic emancipation and were signed by large proportions of leading Protestants, their lordships taking this to show what good relations there were between the religious groups in 1819.[14]

Belfast was also renowned for being antipathetic to slavery; the freed slave Olaudah Equiano during his tour of Ireland in the 1790s had been made particularly welcome in the town.[15] George Benn characterised the petitions on emancipation as 'advances towards reconciliation'.[16] However, the modern historian Jonathan Bardon has suggested that since Protestants formed an overwhelming majority only in this area of Ireland, only here could they safely espouse such a cause, without fears of a Catholic resurgence.[17] The Catholic population of Belfast was less than ten per cent of the whole in 1800. That the proportion began to grow might be seen as a reason why Benn's 'reconciliation' seemed not to last; thirty-four per cent of Belfast's population were Catholic by 1861.[18] Furthermore, liberal views were not universal. Drennan was behind a petition to the Houses of Commons and Lords in 1813 from the Friends of Civil and Religious Liberty and of Internal Peace and Concord. Drawn up after a meeting in the White Linen Hall, the petition had resolved that:

> in the present crisis when the outrageous proceedings of Orangemen threaten so alarmingly to disturb the peace of the country petitions to both Houses of Parliament praying for the suppression of Orange Societies equally with all other illegal associations ought to be immediately put forward.[19]

The Orange Order had been founded in 1795 and in the new century was 'drawn increasingly ... from the poorest social order [and was] regarded by the Presbyterian farmers and the urban middle classes [like Drennan] with contempt'.[20] A few years later news of the failure of the Roman Catholic Relief Bill to pass into law was greeted in the town with 'strong demonstrations of joy', including the burning of tar barrels, firing of guns, and displaying of Orange flags.[21] Such activities were symptomatic of the bitter contestation that plagued Belfast at this period between nationalists and unionists (which, despite the religious adherence of Drennan and others, was largely also between Catholics and Protestants).

84

'The duty of withdrawing from any riotous assembly': the twelfth of July and other celebrations

The conflict was often expressed in street violence, which was associated with both a regular cycle of activities and occasional individual events. Catholics would mark St Patrick's Day and Easter. In 1824 about two thousand Catholics paraded on the saint's day with fifes and drums – but also pistols and bludgeons – and there were riots. Ribbonmen were often present at St Patrick's Day celebrations in Belfast, despite the rural focus of this Catholic society.[22] The *Belfast News Letter* reported in 1843 that Easter Monday had passed peacefully with little drunkenness or disorder and no rioting. The event was 'unattended by the disgraceful scenes which were of so frequent occurrence in former years at the return of this season'.[23] Special constables were sworn in on 16 March 1848 'for the preservation of peace' on the following St Patrick's Day.

It was usually the Protestant, Orange, marches on 12 July, with their 'rafts of rivering flags winding through the streets',[24] that brought most disorder. The battle of the Boyne, which the festival commemorates, took place on 1 July under the Julian calendar and did not become the now familiar date until the Gregorian calendar was adopted. Thus in 1766 the *Belfast News Letter* reported that fireworks were being prepared to celebrate on 1 July next.[25] Some years later the newspaper noted that 'Yesterday, being the first of July [1779], three volunteer companies paraded with orange cockades … in commemoration of the Battle of the Boyne.'[26] A report of the 1797 event estimated attendance at the parade in Belfast to be between six and seven thousand. The spectators:

> assembled at an early hour [and] paraded through the streets with music playing, drums beating and colours flying. On the last were different devices, a painting of King William on horseback etc. … every person in the procession wore orange or blue cockades or ribbands.[27]

In the new century violence often occurred. In 1813 two persons were shot dead when returning from Lisburn to Belfast after what was by now the 12 July parade; 'disgraceful outrages', thundered the *Belfast News Letter*, reporting on a town meeting held later to consider the matter.[28] The next year was 'orderly and quiet' by contrast.[29] In the 1820s the tone of newspaper reports changed, with some implications that the authorities were partial and were condoning the trouble. For example, rioters from 12 July 1825 had their sentences reduced in December by the viceroy, Lord Wellesley.[30] In 1822 *The Times* carried a report from John Lawless, proprietor of *The Irishman* newspaper, to the effect that for twenty-four hours from 3.00 a.m. on 12 July illegal assemblies of Protestants were firing guns and doing all they could to provoke the town's Catholic population. Lawless stated that he personally, together with a Catholic priest, had prevented similar displays by Catholics on St Patrick's Day, so why were disturbances allowed on 12 July?[31] In a similar vein, in 1828, *The Times* repeated an earlier report in the *Northern Whig* about an attack on an Orange lodge returning from an event on Cave Hill. The lodge was confronted by a Catholic group on the Whitehouse Road, egged on by a uniformed sergeant of dragoons. Only the influence of a Catholic bishop, the Right Reverend Dr Crolly, prevented a serious affray.[32]

Four years later, in 1832, it was newsworthy that 12 July passed off reasonably peacefully, although there had been an Orange riot in May.[33] The main parade that year was from Ballymacarrett and had fifty-three lodges, forty-three banners and about seven thousand followers and encountered only some heckling when it passed by Frederick Street. There may have been a particular reason for this relative calm, however, as fears about the cholera epidemic then present in the town kept the crowds down to about a third of their usual size.[34] In 1835 the Catholics of the Pound aped their opponents by erecting a green arch, leading to both Orange and green arches being destroyed by the authorities. Considerable efforts by mounted troops were evidently required to tear down the Orange arch in Sandy Row.[35] A visitor to Belfast in 1837 wrote:

> parties run very high in Belfast; the Protestants being divided among themselves, while the Romish enemy, or rather enmity, is strong in bitterness, though weak in comparative numbers. Such life as the broad thoroughfares present would be highly amusing, did not some bodings of a violent conflict damp that feeling.[36]

This was after the Grand Orange Lodge had dissolved itself in 1836, but in Belfast meetings had continued to be held privately, stoked by fears of Catholic Ribbonism in the town as the number and proportion of Catholics rose given the labour demands of infrastructural investments. Sybil E. Baker noted that whilst Catholics formed 6.5 per cent of the population in the mid-eighteenth century, they formed 31 per cent in 1834 and 43 per cent in 1843:

> the hopes or fears of a Catholic engulfment permeated mid-century Belfast, and helped to explain the violence with which each group sought to establish its territorial dominance.[37]

In 1842 there was 'social tranquillity' on 12 July, perhaps related to the fact that a troop of the eighth Hussars and a hundred extra police from Dublin had been drafted to the town for the event.[38] The next year the Protestant Brethren, then operating as the Belfast Protestant Operatives Society, resolved to 'respect and obey the law against processions on the approaching twelfth of July';[39] even so, there was violence in Sandy Row and Barrack Street, where riots had 'hourly risen'.[40] The following week brought clashes between Protestants from Sandy Row and Catholics attending a burial at the Catholic cemetery at Friar's Bush.[41] The 1835 Municipal Reform Commissioners had noted with distaste the 'melancholy particulars of the "Sandy Row riots", arising out of the unchristian practice of hooting at, insulting, and attacking persons attending the funerals of deceased Roman Catholics'.[42]

In 1845 the *Belfast News Letter* commented with evident satisfaction that the Party Processions Act, which had 'made party processions penal and under the operation of which great numbers of members of Orange Societies were imprisoned is no longer the law of the land'.[43] This granting of legitimacy did not make the renewed marches less controversial and that year the newspaper editorialised that:

> nearly all the nobility and gentry to whom Protestants are accustomed to yield deference and respect are seriously opposed to all processions on the forthcoming 12th.[44]

They were held, nonetheless, but passed off with 'quietness and tranquillity',[45] even though about a thousand militant Catholic

Ribbonmen were thought to be in the town.[46] However, the following year parades held on Monday 13 July saw Orangemen attacked by 'ruffians' from Smithfield and Hercules Street.[47]

The use of street names in this manner was usually sufficient to identify the religious persuasion of working-class people in the town, given Belfast's segregation. Mention of Smithfield, Hercules Street or Pound Street (usually just called the Pound) identified Catholics, whilst Sandy Row was synonymous with Protestants. On occasion, however, the newspaper would give details, as in July 1846, when there was rioting in streets at the northern end of Belfast. Pinkerton's Row was described as 'a locality distinguished as the habitat of Roman Catholic labourers known as mud-larks'. This group had originally been employed on building the new Bridewell and had moved on to labour on the Cave Hill Railway and the Water Works.[48]

In 1847 the *Belfast News Letter* endeavoured 'to dissuade those Protestants ... who propose celebrating ... by a public procession', but to no avail. There was a march, which passed off without incident.[49] Three years later the fact that there had been no trouble accompanying the parades on 12 July was again of sufficient novelty to be reported in *The Times*,[50] but violence continued to flare in other years. In 1852, although parades had been outlawed again with the new Party Processions Act in 1850, tensions were high because of an election and gunfire broke out on 12 July; someone was killed.[51] In 1857:

> on the recommendation of the Mayor, [the Police Affairs Committee] have allowed an additional week's pay to the Day and Night Constables, in consideration of the very arduous duty imposed on them during the disturbed state of the town at and subsequent to the 12th July last.[52]

Rioting continued in the city for months that year, as *The Times* reported twice that September, noting that whilst some Presbyterian ministers had appealed for calm, others had not.[53] On 30 September the town was quieter but unease and resentment stalked the quays and streets.[54] A few days later the newspaper devoted an editorial to the Belfast riots, laying the blame squarely upon the street preaching by a Protestant minister, the Reverend Hugh Hannah, a controversial figure often dubbed 'Roaring Hugh Hanna'. Public ranting in Belfast was nothing unusual in itself. The steps of the Customs House (erected just the year before in 1856) became noted for public address, as celebrated by the modern statue, *The Orator* by Gareth Knowles, which stands upon them (Figure 3.1). This location became the 'storm centre of ranting aggressiveness', where 'the Pope is dethroned, scalped, roasted and consigned to eternal damnation every Sunday afternoon during busy times' as the nationalist Irish expatriate to Argentina, William Bulfin, put it in 1907. Bulfin noted that on occasion 'the audience becomes infuriated and goes up town on the war trail looking for battle'.[55] However, Hanna, it seemed, was ambulatory and his message was not acceptable to many of those who could not help but hear him on the public thoroughfares. *The Times* complained that Hanna didn't stop preaching when the riots started, but kept it up for weeks afterwards.[56] A deputation to the Police Affairs Committee that year pressed for three or four additional lockups to be erected throughout the town, 'where in times of popular excitement persons apprehended might be confined until they could be brought either to the present Police Office or the Petty Sessions Court'.[57] Presumably in the expectation of future violence, in November 1857 the police were issued with 200 wooden batons, purchased at 1s 1d each from a local saw mill.[58]

Another means of crowd control was persuasion. In 1861 the council's Police Committee:

> would suggest to well disposed persons the duty of withdrawing from any riotous assembly, as their presence in such crowds interferes with the efforts of the police to restore order, encourages the rioters, and also exposes themselves to personal injury.[59]

'The excitable character of our operative and labouring classes'

Whilst *The London Review* in 1865 summed up the 12 July festivities generally as a 'saturnalia of bigotry and ruffianism',[60] on occasion a particular incident, rather than a predictable calendar entry, was the catalyst for violence. Sometimes trouble followed in the wake of Daniel O'Connell, the Liberator, a notable figure first in the struggle for Catholic emancipation (achieved in 1829 when Catholic MPs were allowed to sit in the House of Commons, O'Connell being the first) and then in the movement that campaigned for the repeal of the 1801

Figure 3.1 *The Orator*, Customs House steps

Act of Union between Great Britain and Ireland. In December 1840 the *Belfast News Letter* published a letter from O'Connell about a visit to the north.[61] It was suggested that the Protestant clerics Drs Cooke and Montgomery should debate with him face to face on a public platform.[62] Two weeks later the newspaper published a letter from Henry Cooke repeating this challenge, which was not taken up by O'Connell, seemingly on the grounds that Cooke was not a worthy opponent,[63] even though it was later said that Cooke had been responsible for making 'the defence of Protestantism, and not the fraternity of Wolfe Tone, the political shibboleth of Belfast's Noncomformity'.[64] As an aside it might be pointed out that both O'Connell and Cooke ended up with prominent statues standing in

Figure 3.2 Henry Cooke statue

Dublin and Belfast respectively, that of Cooke being erected on the
site in Great Victoria Street previously occupied by the earl of Belfast
(Figure 3.2).[65]

A more practical means of dealing with O'Connell than subjecting
him to debate was to send 800 soldiers from Dublin by steamer. The
Belfast News Letter recommended:

> a powerful force stationed at intervals along the line of the road from
> Banbridge to this town [Belfast], as our information is positive that
> should Mr O'Connell be so ill-advised as to bring a procession with
> him from Newry the worst consequences may be seriously
> apprehended.[66]

In the event, the visit passed off without much violence. The *Belfast News Letter*, not a supporter of O'Connell, commented that 'for once in his life he has displayed a measure of cautious wisdom, for which we are willing to afford him ample credit'.[67] Other meetings were held: students of Royal Belfast College met in the Exchange Buildings[68] and there was a 'great conservative meeting in Wellington Place on Lord Stanley's Bill and Repeal of the Union'.[69] On another occasion, matters were less peaceful: in September 1843 it was announced that there was to be an inquiry led by a magistrate into the repeal riots of July 1842.[70] During the same month the *Belfast News Letter* announced that an anti-repeal declaration was available for signature at its premises in Rosemary Street and also in the Commercial News Room.[71] In 1848 a repeal meeting on St Patrick's Day was abandoned; it had been intended to use it to present sympathy and congratulations to French republicans on the revolution that ended the Orléans monarchy and set up the second republic.[72] Another meeting was held in May in the Repeal Room in Chapel Lane, one report commenting that it had attracted both old and young repealers.[73]

Perhaps the most serious violence in Belfast associated (at least indirectly) with O'Connell occurred in 1864, seventeen years after his death. A private and confidential report on the riots of that year details the circumstances in a factual way without noticeable bias and has been paraphrased below. These particular riots were a reaction to a repeal rally held in Dublin in August.

– 8 August: an attempt by Protestants from Sandy Row to intercept Catholics returning from a rally in Dublin (at which the foundation of O'Connell's statue had been laid), burning an effigy of O'Connell as their train passed by.

– 9 August: the carrying of 'O'Connell's coffin' about Sandy Row. The coffin was then burnt and the ashes cast into the Blackstaff. Another group of Protestants demanded admittance to the Catholic Friar's Bush graveyard to 'bury' O'Connell. A crowd headed towards a Catholic district but were deterred by police.

– 10 August: Catholics wrecked the Falls Road Methodist Chapel. The report helpfully adds in a footnote that 'to "wreck" means to break all the windows with a volley of stones'. Rumours spread that Christ Church was being wrecked and Sandy Row people went there and engaged in stone throwing with 'the Pound mob', who burned straw, saying this was an effigy of William of Orange. Nineteen people from Sandy Row and ten from the Pound were arrested.

- 11 August: mobs assembled, but other than blank shots being fired there was no rioting 'of any moment'.
- 12 August: wrecking of the Catholic Bankmore Penitentiary, Dr Henry Cooke's church and some Protestant houses, with no proof as to which incident happened first.
- 13 and 14 August: the weekend, when, 'quietness prevailed', with trifling property damage only. People wondered if the trouble was over, but it was not.
- 15 August: Lady Day, a Catholic holiday. Several hundred Catholic navvies employed on building new docks assembled at St Malachy's Chapel and marched 'in military order' to Cornmarket, then to Brown Street and Brown Square, where they wrecked Protestant houses and attacked Brown Street School. Workers from the Soho Foundry came out to protect the school and see to any of their children who attended it and drove the navvies away. There were minor incidents as the Catholics dispersed in Millfield and Stanley Street. In the evening a Protestant mob attacked St Malachy's, which was protected by armed Catholics, and shots were fired. The report notes that the navvies were mostly strangers to Belfast and concludes that they were inspired and guided by locals.
- 16 August: the navvies and the Pound mob obtained arms from Smithfield; Protestants including 'Island-men' (Protestant shipyard workers from Queen's Island) did the same at a hardware store in High Street. (Edward Harland later stated that he disapproved of the behaviour of some of his workers and threatened to close the shipyard if any of the few Catholics employed there were turned out.)[74] Riots took place in many areas, occasioning fatalities; robberies occurred.
- 17 August: there was a fight at Thompson's Bank, where many of the navvies worked. Protestants from the shipyards and Coates Foundry proceeded to Thompson's Bank and were fired on and driven off to Ship Street. The Protestants, reinforced and armed, returned to Thompson's Bank and drove the Catholics into the mud, the tide being out. The report goes into much detail, taking evidence from witnesses to indicate that the Catholics were not fired upon whilst in the mud, although stones were thrown and one man was injured by an adze.

— 18 August: the funeral of John McConnell, a Protestant shot by the police and one of nine to die in the riots. The procession, whilst in Donegall Place, was ambushed by Catholics emerging from Hercules Street. Shots were fired in the air but the military intervened and no injuries occurred. The report concludes that the riots ended that day, although there were further assaults and some wrecking of houses the next day. '"Peace meetings" were held and the town gradually assumed its wonted aspect.'

The report goes on to criticise the actions of the military and police who, it seemed, collected in large bodies and could thus be 'easily evaded' by the rioters. The report then critiqued the official Commission of Enquiry. At this point it becomes clear that it was written from a Protestant viewpoint, its earlier depiction of the actual events having been more or less free from overt editorial comment.[75]

After these events in 1864 the police demanded a hundred additional officers to swell their complement of 160 in order to quell riots better. They also requested that the number of police stations be increased from one to three – they should be large stations, too, each with room for thirty officers and fifty prisoners. It was also recommended that 'one hundred and fifty cutlasses be provided, to be used by the force for the suppression of riots, and that the force be properly drilled in the use of this very formidable weapon'. The police suggested that their oversight body, the council's Police Committee, must be:

> well aware of the excitable character of our operative and labouring classes, and the difference in both political and religious views. If the slightest provocation be given on either side, a riot is sure to ensue, as evinced by the late scenes of disorder, which caused the loss of so much life and property in the Town.[76]

If the Police Committee would adopt these recommendations:

> we would be enabled, in the event of a disturbance, to bring in a very short space of time, a force of one hundred well armed men to bear upon the scene, and crush in the bud what might otherwise become a formidable riot.[77]

The London Review concluded that the blame in 1864 lay:

> far more at the door of the Town Council than of the mobs of Pound
> Street and Sandy Row ... They lie contiguous – or, as Mrs Malaprop
> might correctly enough express it – 'contagious' to each other ... and
> the inhabitants, pursuing the occupations of mechanics, mill-workers
> and labourers, have from father to son for many generations eyed
> each other with that thoroughly Christian hatred which exists in its
> perfection in the North of Ireland in general and in the respectable
> town of Belfast in particular. The Pound has only to frown at Sandy
> Row or Sandy Row to 'bite its thumb' at the Pound and both
> neighbourhoods are up in arms. Woe then to the rest of the
> community. Chapels and churches are wrecked, schools and
> penitentiaries. From stones the contending mobs fly to bludgeons,
> and from bludgeons to pistols and guns. Shops are closed and trade
> stands still, the inhabitants shut themselves up in their houses and
> remain there in fear and trembling. Now in one quarter of the town,
> now in another, the tide of riot surges to and fro, as each party for
> the moment gains the upper hand. And while dead bodies are being
> carried back to their homes and wounded ones to the hospitals, a
> handful of police rush from place to place making bad worse by their
> evident helplessness to stem the torrent, much less to force it back.
> Such is the state of things which the industrial capital of Ireland has
> more than once witnessed and will witness assuredly yet again, unless
> a little common sense can be driven into the head of the Town
> Council, at once the most feeble and most mischievous body to
> which the safe keeping of a community was ever committed.[78]

The London Review went on to recommend that Belfast's police force
be strengthened and that its procedures be revised, including removing
control of the police from the town council – as did the Commission
of Enquiry.[79] This happened a few months later in September 1865.
That there were only five Catholic police officers was another matter
needing to be addressed. As it was, 'the riots of 1857 [had been]
repeated in the riots of 1864, and we know not the hour when Belfast
may be again the scene of conflicts equally savage, bloody and stupid'.[80]
In fact, there were 'very serious riots' in the summer of 1872,[81] after the
Party Processions Act of 1850 had been repealed and Orange marches

had recommenced. The Catholics countered with their own 'March to Hannahstown', which erupted into violence lasting almost a fortnight. Baker concluded:

> It required 2,000 extra police and military, the Inspector General, four magistrates, the closure of the public houses, the banning of the sale of firearms, and finally the exhaustion of the rioters to restore calm.[82]

The council minutes later reported that the riots had come to the attention of parliament.[83]

Altercations happened also in 1880 and 1884. Mark Radford has written an article about riots in 1886 in which thirty-two people died, hundreds were injured and £90,000 worth of damage was caused. That year Home Rule tensions were high and an argument between Catholics and Protestants at the docks in early June sparked six days of rioting. The 12 July festivities set off another three days of riots, with a more protracted period of strife from 31 July until 21 September. Armed police reinforcements were required, supported by troops, and twenty-four of the deaths were of people shot by the police. Rioters' weapons included stones from the roads, especially 'kidney pavers', and Belfast or Queen's Island 'confetti': rivets, screws, metal scrap (rovings) and other items stolen from the shipyards and often propelled by catapult.

Sir Edward Harland was the mayor at this time and so was directly concerned in these affairs. He denied that his shipyard was sectarian. There were 225 Catholics working there at this time out of a workforce of three thousand, but 190 of them stopped attending work during the riots and early in the following year only 77 had gone back.[84] It is known that Harland and Wolff had plans to leave Ireland had Home Rule been granted.[85] Actions during the riots included the 'Battle of Bowershill', largely involving Protestants against the police, and the 'Battle of Springfield', a gun battle between Catholics and Protestants. The government's Riots Commission laid the blame on clergymen and politicians who had spoken of violence as a way of resisting Home Rule. Police tactics also came in for criticism.[86]

'Ruffianism and respectability may become fused by party heat': elections and local politics

Another opportunity for violence was electioneering; the Municipal Reform Commissioners described 'the collision of the exasperated parties on the occasion of the chairing of the Members for the borough after the general election in December 1832' as the 'Hercules Street riots'.[87] In the general election of 1841 letters from candidates to the electors were published,[88] along with verbatim reports of candidates' speeches, including those of James Emerson Tennant.[89] However, this election was noted more for deeds than words. A rally had to be relocated to the Gymnasium in Fountain Street because the chosen venue, the Circus in Wellington Place, had to undergo repairs 'in consequence of the accident which happened at their last night of meeting'.[90] The Circus served also as the camp for troops of the tenth Royal Hussars from Dublin, who had been brought north to provide security for the nomination held at the Courthouse on 6 July. The hussars and two hundred officers from the county constabulary, added to the local police, made up a contingent of upwards of a thousand men.[91] The election was won by the Conservative candidates, Tennant and William Johnston.[92] In 1842 Tennant and James Ross were elected[93] after a campaign noted in *The Times* as having been characterised by 'gross bribery and extensive corruption'.[94]

Indeed, Belfast became notorious for election violence alongside and associated with sectarian violence, meriting a long article in *The London Review* in 1865:

> Should anyone wish to learn how ruffianism and respectability may become fused by party heat so that it shall become impossible to distinguish between the gentleman and the blackguard, let him read the accounts of the election for Belfast, the most prosperous and ill-behaved town in Ireland.[95]

The anonymous author admitted that there were some riots in English elections, but claimed that there the bludgeon had been laid aside as a party weapon. This was 'not so in Belfast':

> There an inclination to violence is the normal condition of the public mind ... the smouldering fire of political and religious strife blazes up and rages with more or less violence at least once a year.[96]

The violence at the nomination of candidates for the election of 1865 was then described when Lord John Hay, who stood for the Liberals, was threatened by Orangemen, 'each flourishing a bludgeon or "skullcracker" [and whilst] Orange bludgeons had signalized the day of nomination, Orange ditties were to celebrate the day of declaration'.[97] At the count a 'mob in the court house' sang 'Derry's Walls', 'The Orange and the Blue' and 'No Surrender' and the chair, a Mr Kane (perhaps a young Dr Richard Rutledge Kane, later minister of Christ Church), delivered a 'wanton and insulting tirade' denigrating the Catholic religion. The correspondent, no supporter of the Orange cause, concluded:

> the town of Belfast prides itself on its progress and enlightenment and, as far as progress goes, its boast must be admitted. But how is its enlightenment consistent with the fact that in respect of political and religious intolerance it is the plague-spot of Ireland and a disgrace to the civilization of the United Kingdom[?][98]

The correspondent was particularly upset by the fact that a portion of 'the gentility of Belfast' joined in:

> the rioters of Sandy Row can reckon with certainty on the sympathy and connivance of Tory gentlemen, of Tory magistrates and their police ... What but periodical riot and bloodshed can be expected from the scum of the town when a considerable proportion of its elite inhabitants place themselves on a level with the scum and act as their fuglemen [ringleaders][?][99]

Class strife was somewhat obscured behind Belfast's ethnic troubles, but on occasion it would come to the fore, for the class divisions were marked. O'Hanlon, himself English, stated in 1853:

> the contrasts which glare out upon the eye as it descends from the summit to the base of the social fabric here is [sic] stronger than I remember to have seen it in any other locality.[100]

There were class-based riots in Belfast in protest at the Corn Laws in 1815.[101] Almost a century later, in 1907, there were labour disputes over low wages, which transcended sectarian divisions, uniting members of the Catholic and Protestant working classes. This included the actions of James Larkin (another person who went on to be memorialised – Larkin's statue is in O'Connell Street, Dublin) at the docks. John Gray has charted the actions of the 1907 dock strike and the violent reaction to it by the authorities, which led to a police mutiny. In the end the strikers and Larkin 'faced final defeat on the coal quays at Belfast' and Gray noted that 'opportunities for real social advance, albeit with attendant political risks were lost, and they remained trapped instead in a barren oscillation between the twin poles of proletarianism and sectarianism'.[102]

In its 1908 report the Linen Merchants' Association noted they would be:

> sorry to appear to endorse the Socialist doctrine that capital and labour were natural enemies. There were exceptions to every rule, but [the Linen Merchants' Association] did not believe that employers as a whole had any desire to deal unfairly or oppressively by their workers, any more than these workers, if free from the interference of professional agitators, had any desire to demand unreasonable or impossible terms from their employers. Unfortunately during the past year the professional trouble-maker had been busy amongst them ... the result has been ... to make employers draw closer together, and to feel that what concerned one concerned all.[103]

A little earlier, in 1906, the Linen Merchants' Association had been in dispute about overtime working and had felt that 'The interference of Belfast Trades Council [was] the usual gratuitous kind.'[104]

A different level of politics was the local council, which was mired in financial scandal in the nineteenth century. In 1848, for example, there was an involved case concerning property valuations and the rights these conferred regarding voting for the Belfast Harbour Commissioners. The commissioners accused the town council of deliberately valuing properties of one group too low so as to deprive their owners of votes.[105] In 1856 *The Times* reported that Belfast Corporation was insolvent,[106] and three years later there was a commission of inquiry 'into the state of municipal affairs of the borough of Belfast'.[107] Later, the former town solicitor was accused of collusion in covering up the financial misdeeds of previous councillors.[108]

Another frequent concern was the council's own premises. On 1 November 1842 the first meeting of the new Belfast Corporation was held in the Town Hall,[109] but less than two years later the General Purposes Committee was 'engaged in making arrangements for a place of meeting for the council and ascertaining the probable outlay attendant on it',[110] but at the following meeting it seemed clear that this would be in the existing premises, albeit fitted up 'in a suitable manner for the meetings of the council'.[111] In 1863 the council again appointed a committee to look into finding a new place for council meetings,[112] and later decided to build a new town hall.[113] Whilst the council set aside £15,000 for the project, it acknowledged that 'the cost of erecting a handsome and commodious Town Hall will probably be not less than £25,000', with an additional £5,000 if the Central Police Office and Petty Sessions Courthouse were to be erected on the same site.[114] By 1870 the building, on Victoria Street, was well under

Figure 3.3 Belfast Town Hall, Victoria Street

Figure 3.4 Belfast City Hall, Donegall Square

way and the council's Town Hall Committee was much exercised with its heating arrangements.[115] A year later it was reported that the building would be ready for use the following month (Figure 3.3).[116]

In due course having a mere town hall would become inappropriate, for the council was set on a higher status for Belfast. In 1887 they sent a memorial to the lord lieutenant petitioning for the town to be created a city.[117] This request was granted in 1888. The first mention of the town hall's replacement, Belfast City Hall, came on 16 November 1889, when it was announced that the site of the White Linen Hall in Donegall Square would used.[118] A budget of £120,000 was established in 1893, which the council expected to be met by rents from the municipal tram system.[119] A competition for designs opened on 1 July 1896[120] and Belfast City Hall, whose architect was Alfred Brumwell Thomas, opened in 1906 (Figure 3.4).

The council was unionist, of course, and loyal, although in 1840 money that would have been spent on illuminating the town on the occasion of Queen Victoria's marriage was devoted instead to the funds of the General and Fever Hospital.[121] By contrast, in 1863, a generation later, £24 8s 11d was spent on illuminating the town hall to celebrate the marriage of the prince of Wales. Thrift remained in evidence, however, as a proposal to spend an additional £100 on fireworks was not adopted.[122] In 1872 the mayor reported with evident satisfaction that he had attended a thanksgiving service in the cathedral for the restoration to health of the prince of Wales and had been allocated one of the best seats. From there he had witnessed 'hearty and united demonstrations of loyalty ... anything to the contrary would be but as a single drop in the ocean of loyalty that had been manifested in every part of the United Kingdom'.[123] Despite its hard line on allegiance to the crown, on occasion the council displayed liberal attitudes – for example, when it petitioned parliament in favour of the Women's Suffrage Bill in June 1872.[124]

Loyalty was manifested also in attitudes to Home Rule. There was a special meeting of the council in 1893, at which it was stated that Home Rule would be 'ruinous to Ireland and disastrous to Great Britain'.[125] Furthermore, that year the Belfast Chamber of Commerce had supplied written evidence to Prime Minister Gladstone regarding the Government of Ireland Bill of 1893; a deputation from the chamber met with Gladstone. The records of that meeting reveal it to have been a tense affair, the views of the protagonists about Home Rule differing. Gladstone had read the chamber's report and was not keen on also having to listen to its authors. No less a delegate than Sir Edward Harland MP intervened and insisted on a longer hearing for the Belfast deputation – using an appropriate engineering metaphor: 'Mr Gladstone's hand [was] pressing, with all gentleness, yet firmly on the throttle-valve of free speech deliverance.'[126] Gladstone himself spoke for half of the one-hour time slot and was pressed to receive a further communication in writing. This lengthy document opined that Home Rule would result in 'confusion and disaster'.[127]

In 1886 the Linen Merchants' Association had presented an address to the prince of Wales giving a 'cordial welcome [to] Your Royal

Highness and the Princess of Wales to Belfast, the capital of Ulster and the centre of the linen trade'.[128] In 1903 the Linen Merchants' Association joined the Flax Spinners' Association, the Flax Supply Association and the Power Loom Manufacturers' Association to welcome Edward VII to Belfast, assuring him of their 'heartiest devotion' and 'unswerving loyalty'.[129] Yet in 1913, the Linen Merchants' Association stated very firmly:

> The Association is non-political, yet I know no member of it who does not feel that the fate of the Linen Trade of Ireland is involved in the question of Home Rule. Our business interests are so deeply affected and so seriously threatened that we cannot exclude the subject from our consideration. Acting on this conviction, [a delegation was] appointed by your Council to represent this Association on the Deputation of the Belfast Chamber of Commerce which waited upon Mr. Asquith on the 10th July in the House of Commons. The object of the Deputation was to place before the Prime Minister the reasons for our determined opposition to Home Rule on purely commercial grounds.[130]

'Intestine broils': Catholic–Protestant relations

Belfast was not in riot all the time. On most days its groups had to find a way of dealing with their rivals without violence. Separation and segregation must have helped quietude – often the opposing side's absence meant that there could be no direct antagonism. Anthony C. Hepburn and Brenda Collins have identified very high levels of segregation for 1901, especially in working-class Catholic areas such as the Falls, the Pound and Ardoyne. There was less extreme segregation in working-class Protestant areas, whilst middle-class areas were more mixed still, but to some extent the Protestant domination of these districts was masked by the presence of Catholic domestic servants.[131] For those whose residential location did not protect them from potential unpleasant interaction, other tactics might have to be adopted, including simply hiding away, as evoked in W.R. Rodgers's portrait of his Mountpottinger childhood in *The return room*:

Shipyard horn, prolonged
NARRATOR
That was the resurrection sound which wakened me each morning –
the Island horn. And in the dark of a winter's morning I could hear
the tramp of hundreds of feet going past to their lives in the shipyard.

   Mrs Mulligan, a mile away, crossed herself uneasily as the
Protestant feet tramped past her house. And her twelve children fell
quiet under the bedclothes, for fear the feet might quicken and break
into a run.[132]

The sound of feet was evocative of Belfast in the words of another
significant writer on the city, the geographer Emrys Jones. Describing
working-class Belfast, he recorded:

   the physical environment is of a distinctive kind, and when it is
   brought alive it is to the sound of factory workers' boots, the clamour
   of children and the talking of shawled women.[133]

Catholic and Protestants usually lived in different areas of the town
(city) and many would not have met their rivals even at work. Those
who worked in the shipyards, for example, as noted, were almost
exclusively Protestant. This was not true of the linen industry, but one
man whose long career in that industry started in 1903 reported that
there was little trouble at work:

   the female mill workers, spinners etc. were predominantly Catholics,
   and the factory workers (weavers etc) about 75 percent Protestants,
   all working harmoniously together until the partition of Ireland.[134]

This caveat presumably was added in light of an incident he related for
the early 1920s 'when some of the militant "prods" tried to get the
"mickeys" expelled, the Protestants being in the majority'. However:

   the foreman acted diplomatically ... contacted the ringleader and
   ... said the Catholics had to live as well as the Protestants. So ended
   a situation which might have developed and become serious.[135]

There is some insightful detail on the humdrum, quotidian
relationships between Protestants and Catholics in primary data,

including accounts from two men who kept journals of their movements around Belfast in the 1850s: Reverend William O'Hanlon, a Congregationalist and, especially, Reverend Anthony McIntyre, a Unitarian. McIntyre was in the employment of the Unitarian Domestic Mission to the Poor of Belfast and his journal was prepared for the mission;[136] O'Hanlon wrote a series of articles for the *Northern Whig*, later collected into a book.[137]

McIntyre was very much the stern Protestant clergyman. On one visit he praised a respectable widow, Mrs McKenna of Lower Kent Street, who had 'wrought for some years since the death of her husband to keep the children and herself out of the workhouse and she has succeeded'. By contrast, on the way to Mrs McKenna's room, McIntyre passed the door of a family that enjoyed three times her income but 'these people are as miserable and degraded as the others are comfortable and respectable'.[138] Whilst acknowledging that the man of the degraded family drank, the principal reason given for the contrast was:

> in the one family the Sabbath is observed, the Bible and other good works are read. In the other the Sabbath is made the most sinful day of the seven, no Bible in the house.[139]

Another common cause of distress to McIntyre was the behaviour of the Catholics he encountered or heard about. In September 1853 in Samuel Street he met with Mary Kirk, a Presbyterian widow, who complained of the unregulated Sabbath behaviour of some of her (nominally Catholic) neighbours, for 'no person visits these families except the priest who comes sometimes (she believes for money)'.[140]

McIntyre was prepared to visit Catholics himself, but was also willing to record his antipathy when he did so, especially regarding a shoemaker called Megarry who was 'a bigoted papist' who held that only Catholics could be saved, which had led to 'a long discussion'.[141] Towards the end of his journal in 1856 McIntyre recounted the story of a Catholic mother in Coar's Lane whose 'little boy had attended the Catholic school for a length of time in Donegall Street and had learned nothing' but now he was at the William Street school 'he is most anxious to get away in the morning. Very many have unsolicitedly made similar statements.'[142] In March 1854 McIntyre had been checking on children who had missed school and was told by one mother that she had withdrawn her two children after their schoolmaster had torn pieces of shamrock from their clothing when they had arrived at school so decorated on St Patrick's Day. McIntyre, when he checked, was assured that this was not the case.[143]

One boy who had applied to attend McIntyre's school for a few weeks before his family emigrated to America was the child of a Catholic mother, who had:

> a great deal … of the superstitious savage in her. She … received me very civilly, but I have little hope that much could be made of her or of her child while he is under her control. She threw a can of water at Mr Graham, scripture reader of the General Assembly, one day because he proposed to read scripture with her, and she told him that if ever he would dare to call again it would not be a cold but a hot bath he would get.[144]

Her boy was allowed to remain at school 'for the purpose of trying whether any impression can be made on so savage a nature'.[145]

Another Catholic family had removed their boys from the school but after two months wanted them to be readmitted. McIntyre refused on the grounds that no good reason had been given for their removal, but then met the eldest in Donegall Street, finding him 'dirty, ragged and dejected'. It seemed that the boy had left the school after being involved in a plot to beat the teacher, but he protested his innocence and McIntyre readmitted him on condition of better conduct. There was an implication that his mother had been influenced by 'interested parties', which explained the boy's behaviour.[146]

In 1855 McIntyre carried out visits in Sandy Row, where 'a very strong party feeling exists'.[147] As O'Hanlon added, it was the haunt of the 'bludgeon-men' and he entered the street only with trepidation, though nothing amiss ever happened to him.[148] McIntyre wrote:

> Mrs McKibbin told me that a few days previous a woman who is a Protestant herself and whose husband went to no place of worship, but who ought to have been a Roman Catholic, had allowed him to be buried by the Catholics and that while the funeral was passing along the street the women and girls had gathered and were likely to

pull the priests off the car ... there is such a bitter spirit of hatred between the Protestants and Catholics.[149]

O'Hanlon had 'avoided in these letters any discussion which might be calculated to stir up strife amongst the different sections of the professing church'. Following his own visit to Sandy Row, however, he was moved to write, 'Oh, my country! When wilt thou learn to feel that only shame and ruin can spring from thy intestine broils[?]'[150]

Not all was hatred. McIntyre told of the friendship between an elderly Presbyterian widow, Sally Love, and her neighbour in Grattan Place, Sarah Loughrie, a Catholic, thirty-seven years widowed and 'still more straitened in her circumstances than even Sally'. McIntyre explained that 'though the one is a Presbyterian and the other a Catholic ... yet their hearts appear kind to one another as were the hearts of Saul and Jonathan'.[151] He also wrote of a little girl called Brown, a Protestant orphan, who was cared for by an old Catholic woman and whom he was trying to have placed in the industrial school.[152] For his part, O'Hanlon described Davison's Court off Durham Street, where Mr Davison, an enlightened landlord whose 'power [was] exercised in the most salutary form', ensured that the houses were kept clean and in good order, creating a 'vision of Dante's paradise after walking through his inferno'. Here 'Protestants and Roman Catholics [were] living in perfect harmony': 'Landlords, here is a great moral.'[153]

Nonetheless, it was a rare moral: one Londoner who had lived in Belfast for twelve years reported to an English rector in the late 1870s:

I'd leave it [Belfast] tomorrow if I could ... for it does grieve me ... to see how my children are growing up – Orange ... in spite of me ... I'm in the shop all day, and the mother, she's busy, and they learn of the other children ... I'm quite sure if the school teachers were to set themselves against these things they might teach the children different. But they don't; they encourage them, that's the worst of it.[154]

This English shopkeeper then went on to relate how he had been criticised on his migration voyage across to Ireland for taking a drink 'with a Papist, that's a Roman Catholic; and never you have anything to do with them so long as you're in this country'. He concluded:

Now there is the secret of the Belfast riots; the working men are held from making friends as other working men do, and the minds of the young people are poisoned, and thus the betterment which must come from people working together and getting to feel that they have interests in common, is hindered.[155]

One Belfast exile was even harder on the city. James Douglas, who was Belfast born but had a career as a newspaperman in London, published a book called *The unpardonable sin* about his home city in 1907. That Belfast is dubbed 'Bigotsborough' indicates his attitude:

For generations it has been remarkable for two things, namely revivals of religion and revivals of rioting. It is the city of riots and religions. It may seem absurd to suggest that there is any connection between its love of religion and its love of rioting, but I am sure that both are produced by the same cause. Bigotsborough is a city which suffers from unsatisfied aspirations and baffled aims. Its imagination is starved and it is oppressed by an intolerably grey monotony. It is the loneliest city in the world. It would be happy if it were on the Clyde for its blood is Scottish. But it lives in exile amongst an alien race. It has ceased to be Scottish and is too proud to be Irish.[156]

NOTES

1   *BNL*, 18 January 1780, 8 February 1780.
2   Proclamation by the lord lieutenant, 11 March 1793 (BL, Peel papers, cl, Add MS 40330, f. 183).
3   Ibid.
4   *The Times*, 20 March 1793.
5   *BNL*, 29 May 1798, 17 July 1798.
6   *The Times*, 11 June 1798, 24 July 1798.
7   James Adair Pilson, *History of the rise and progress of Belfast, and annals of the County Antrim* (Belfast, 1846), p. 23.
8   *The Times*, 17 August 1798.
9   Ibid., 28 August 1798; *BNL*, 21 August 1798.
10 *BNL*, 2 January 1801.
11 *The Times*, 1 August 1803.
12 *BNL*, 23 January 1795.
13 *The Times*, 1 December 1818.

14   Ibid., 23 March 1819.
15   Nini Rodgers, *Equiano and anti-slavery in eighteenth-century Belfast* (Belfast, 2000).
16   Benn, *History of the town of Belfast*, p. 59.
17   Jonathan Bardon, *An interesting and honourable history: the Belfast Charitable Society, the first 250 years, 1752–2002* (Belfast, 2002), p. 21.
18   Hepburn and Collins, 'Industrial society'.
19   Printed petition to the House of Lords and the House of Commons, 1813 (BL, Peel papers, l, Add MS 40230, f. 136).
20   Sybil E. Baker, 'Orange and green: Belfast, 1832–1912' in H.J. Dyos and Michael Wolff (eds), *The Victorian city: images and realities* (London, 1973), ii, pp. 789–814.
21   *The Times*, 30 May 1825.
22   *BNL*, 23 March 1824, 26 March 1824.
23   Ibid., 18 April 1843.
24   Rodgers, *Return room*, p. 71.
25   *BNL*, 27 June 1766.
26   Ibid., 2 July 1779.
27   Ibid., 14 July 1797.
28   Ibid., 13 July 1813, 30 July 1813.
29   Ibid., 15 July 1814.
30   *The Times*, 28 December 1825.
31   Ibid., 21 August 1822.
32   Ibid., 18 April 1828.
33   *BNL*, 22 May 1832.
34   *The Times*, 17 July 1832.
35   *BNL*, 14 July 1835, 17 July 1835.
36   Charlotte Elizabeth (Mrs C.E. Tonna), *Letters from Ireland 1837* (London, 1838), p. 332.
37   Baker, 'Orange and green', p. 793.
38   *BNL*, 12 July 1842, 16 July 1842.
39   Ibid., 7 July 1843.
40   Ibid., 18 July 1843.
41   Ibid., 25 July 1843. See also Baker, 'Orange and green'.
42   *Appendix to the first report of the commissioners appointed to inquire into the Municipal Corporations in Ireland* [27], H.C. 1835, xxxvii, 199.
43   *BNL*, 20 June 1845.
44   Ibid., 8 July 1845.
45   Ibid., 15 July 1845.
46   Baker, 'Orange and green'.
47   *BNL*, 14 July 1846.
48   Ibid., 17 July 1846.
49   Ibid., 9 July 1847, 13 July 1847.
50   *The Times*, 15 July 1852.
51   *Northern Whig*, 15 July 1852.
52   BCM, 1 September 1857 (PRONI, LA/7/2/EA/5).
53   *The Times*, 12 September 1857, 15 September 1857.
54   Ibid., 30 September 1857.
55   William Bulfin, *Rambles in Eirinn* (Dublin, 1907), p. 128. See also P. Callan, 'Rambles in Éirinn, by William Bulfin' in *Studies: An Irish Quarterly Review*, lxxi, no. 284 (winter 1982), pp. 391–8.
56   *The Times*, 8 October 1857.
57   BCM, 1 September 1857 (PRONI, LA/7/2/EA/5).

58 Ibid., 2 November 1857.
59 BCM, 2 September 1861 (PRONI, LA/7/2/EA/6).
60 Anon, 'Belfast Tories' in *The London Review* (22 July 1865), p. 82.
61 *BNL*, 15 December 1840.
62 Ibid., 1 January 1841.
63 Ibid., 15 January 1841.
64 Baker, 'Orange and green', p. 790.
65 BCM, 1 August 1874 (PRONI, LA/7/2/EA/11); BCM, 1 April 1876 (PRONI, LA/7/2/EA/12).
66 *BNL*, 15 January 1841.
67 Ibid., 19 January 1841.
68 Ibid.
69 Ibid., 21 January 1841.
70 Ibid., 15 September 1843.
71 Ibid., 12 September 1843.
72 Ibid., 21 March 1848.
73 Ibid., 23 May 1848.
74 Belfast Riots Commission, *Report of the Belfast Riots Commissioners: presented to both houses of parliament by command of her majesty* (London, 1887).
75 Anon, *Statement in reference to the O'Connell procession in Dublin and the riots in Belfast* (Belfast, 1865).
76 BCM, 1 November 1864 (PRONI, LA/7/2/EA/7).
77 Ibid.
78 Anon, 'The borough of Belfast' in *The London Review* (1 April 1865), pp. 345–6.
79 *Report of the commissioners of inquiry, 1864, respecting the magisterial and police jurisdiction, arrangements and establishment for the borough of Belfast* [3466], H.C. 1865, xxviii, 27.
80 Anon, 'Borough of Belfast'.
81 BCM, 1 October 1872 (PRONI, LA/7/2/EA/10).
82 Baker, 'Orange and green', p. 798.
83 BCM, 16 January 1873 (PRONI, LA/7/2/EA/10).
84 Belfast Riots Commission, *Report*.
85 Moss and Hume, *Shipbuilders to the world*.
86 Mark Radford, '"Closely akin to actual warfare": the Belfast riots of 1886 and the RIC' in *History Ireland*, vii, no. 4 (winter 1999), pp. 27–31. See also *Illustrated London News*, 21 August 1886.
87 *Municipal Corporations in Ireland*. See also the detailed description in Baker, 'Orange and green'.
88 *BNL*, 15 June 1841.
89 Ibid., 22 June 1841, 25 June 1841.
90 Ibid., 2 July 1841.
91 Ibid., 6 July 1841.
92 Ibid., 13 July 1841.
93 Ibid., 23 August 1841.
94 *The Times*, 28 July 1842.
95 Anon, 'Belfast Tories'.
96 Ibid.
97 Ibid.
98 Ibid.
99 Ibid.
100 O'Hanlon, *Walks among the poor*, p. 49.

101 *BNL*, 21 March 1815.
102 John Gray, *City in revolt: James Larkin and the Belfast dock strike of 1907* (Belfast, 1985), pp. 191, 209.
103 Annual report of the LMA, 1908 (PRONI, D2088/11/2.)
104 Ibid., 1906.
105 BCM, 1 August 1848 (PRONI, LA/7/2/EA/2).
106 *The Times*, 24 December 1856.
107 *Report of the commissioners appointed to inquire into the state of municipal affairs of the borough of Belfast in Ireland* [2470], H.C. & H.L. 1859, xii, 305.
108 BCM, 1 August 1864 (PRONI, LA/7/2/EA/7).
109 BCM, 1 November 1842 (PRONI, LA/7/2/EA/1).
110 Ibid., 1 July 1844.
111 Ibid., 1 August 1844.
112 BCM, 2 November 1863 (PRONI, LA/7/2/EA/6).
113 BCM, 1 February 1866 (PRONI, LA/7/2/EA/7).
114 Ibid., 1 April 1866.
115 BCM, 1 October 1870 (PRONI, LA/7/2/EA/9).
116 Ibid., 1 September 1871.
117 BCM, 13 June 1887 (PRONI, LA/7/2/EA/16).
118 BCM, 16 November 1889 (PRONI, LA/7/2/EA/17).
119 BCM, 1 February 1893 (PRONI, LA/7/2/EA/19).
120 BCM, 1 July 1896 (PRONI, LA/7/2/EA/20).
121 O'Neill, 'Sanitary science', p. 40.
122 BCM, 7 March 1863 (PRONI, LA/7/2/EA/6).
123 BCM, 1 March 1872 (PRONI, LA/7/2/EA/10).
124 Ibid., 1 May 1872.
125 BCM, 17 April 1893 (PRONI, LA/7/2/EA/19).
126 Belfast Chamber of Commerce, *Mr Gladstone's speech to the Belfast Chamber of Commerce and the chamber's reply* (Belfast, 1893), p. 4.
127 Ibid., p. 26.
128 Annual report of the LMA, 1886 (PRONI, D2088/11/2).
129 Ibid., 1904.
130 Annual report of the LMA, 1913 (PRONI, D2088/11/33).
131 Hepburn and Collins, 'Industrial society'.
132 Rodgers, *Return room*, p. 34.
133 Jones, 'Social geography', p. 9. See also idem, *A social geography of Belfast* (Oxford, 1960).
134 Topping, Memoirs.
135 Ibid.
136 Reverend Anthony McIntyre, Diary kept by the Reverend Anthony McIntyre, 1853–6 (PRONI, D1558/2/3).
137 O'Hanlon, *Walks among the poor*.
138 McIntyre, Diary, p. 14.
139 Ibid.
140 Ibid., p. 22.
141 Ibid., p. 71.
142 Ibid., p. 352.
143 Ibid., p. 128.
144 Ibid., p. 159.
145 Ibid.
146 Ibid., p. 239.

147 Ibid., pp. 292–3.
148 O'Hanlon, *Walks among the poor*, p. 33.
149 McIntyre, Diary, pp. 292–3.
150 O'Hanlon, *Walks among the poor*, pp. 160, 33.
151 McIntyre, Diary, p. 19.
152 Ibid., p. 79.
153 O'Hanlon, *Walks among the poor*, p. 31.
154 Henry Stuart Fagan, *Orange Ulster* (London, 1879), p. 520.
155 Ibid., p. 521.
156 James Douglas, *The unpardonable sin* (Belfast, 1907) (cited in Patricia Craig (ed.), *The Belfast anthology* (Belfast, 1999)).

4

'THE INHABITANTS OF THIS TOWN ARE INDUSTRIOUS AND CAREFUL. BUT METHINKS NOT SO SOCIABLE AS IN OTHER PLACES'[1]

'Lounging blackguards' and 'vagabond ballad singers': the need for social control

One mid-nineteenth-century observer considered that the condition of the 'lowest poor' in Belfast was not likely to be worse than that in other parts of the British Empire, although the gulf between rich and poor was wide.[2] Thus, the poor would not have attended the fancy-dress ball at the Exchange Buildings in 1823, which was reserved for 'notable residents'.[3] The local newspaper actually referred to the 'lower orders' (and their immorality) in 1821,[4] further complaining about 'idle vagabonds' who assembled daily outside the new markets to play pitch and toss – 'where does the money come from which is spent in gambling?';[5] about 'lounging blackguards' that infested Cornmarket;[6] about 'ragamuffins' in Hammond's Court;[7] and about 'idle fellows' playing ball and throwing missiles in York Street.[8] In the same year it was reported that a group of idle boys were seen 'abusing the Sabbath' by playing pitch and toss and the police were sent to stop them.[9] Also on the street were to be found 'vagabond ballad singers vociferating profane and obnoxious songs, to the very great injury of the morals of the rising generation'.[10]

Belfast people proved easy to excite into violence even without reference to their sectarianism – as in 1822, when a schoolmaster was beaten up by a mob in Grattan Street after a lad, perhaps in revenge for some incident at school, had spread a rumour that the man was a child kidnapper.[11] Even innocent events could cause trouble. In 1825, such was the tumult from crowds gathered to gaze upon two visiting Malays that shopkeepers complained that they were unable to hear their customers.[12] Exhibiting foreigners to public gaze seems to have been quite a common amusement: 'Esquimaux Indians from the frozen regions of the north' performed surprising feats in their canoe in the docks in 1822,[13] and later that year a 'savage' chief and his wife from the interior of South America were exhibited.[14] The public was also given the opportunity to turn its gaze on 'a surprising tall man … also a most curious perfect woman in miniature … 32 inches high'.[15] Other exotic amusements included 'a curious performance of rope dancing' at the Market House in 1761[16] and a tightrope act at the same venue in 1773.[17] Mr Lee Sugg, ventriloquist, appeared in 1800;[18] a circus visited in 1801 with 'twelve of the most capital performers in Europe'.[19] There was horse racing at Ballyhackamore in east Belfast.[20] A balloonist came in 1784, announcing that subscribers might 'have the pleasure of jaunting in the aerial chariot'.[21]

It would have been less exhilarating, but safer, later to watch the Belfast Pedestrian, William McNamara, perform feats such as trundling a wheelbarrow on Cromac Bridge for twenty-four hours. McNamara had originally proposed to perambulate around the White Linen Hall, but the wealthy residents of Donegall Square had objected and he had had to remove to a less salubrious part of town.[22] However, a race around the White Linen Hall between a man of seventy carrying a sack weighing 10st 7lb (66.7 kilogrammes) and a young man was allowed to take place. The old man, who had to go round just once compared to the young man's twice, won the prize of twenty guineas.[23] Much childhood leisure took place in the street. W.R. Rodgers, in his evocation of childhood in the 1920s, wrote of:

> boys playing 'piggy' or trundling hoops, or trinkling marbles along the gutter, or speelying up lamposts, or blowing cigarette cards. Everything had its pace and season. The girls this day were skipping and singing as usual.[24]

There were also opportunities for spending leisure time in self-improvement in Belfast, dubbed the "Athens of the North" because of the literary and scientific achievements of a section of its people'.[25]

One outlet was the Belfast Reading Society of 1788, forerunner of the Belfast Library and Society for Promoting Knowledge, which ran a subscription library for its members. The original society was not reserved for the 'notable citizens'; rather, some of its members were 'worthy plebians [*sic*]'. Its founders included a tanner, a gunsmith and a printer as well as professionals such as Roger Mulholland, the architect of the White Linen Hall. However, bankers, merchants and the shipbuilder William Ritchie began to tilt the membership list away from the plebeians in short order. Another tradition amongst members was radicalism; early membership overlapped with that of the Society for United Irishmen. The librarian Thomas Russell and member Henry Joy McCracken were involved in the 1798 rebellion, following which McCracken was hanged (Figure 4.1) and Russell and several others imprisoned. Other members held opposing political viewpoints and remained loyal to the crown.

The society survived such serious rifts and self-improvement remained its watchword. The library was forbidden by statute from purchasing novels. One notable early achievement of the society, by then known as the Belfast Society for Promoting Knowledge, was to arrange a festival of Irish harp music in the Assembly Rooms in 1792.

Figure 4.1 McCracken graves, Clifton Street Cemetery

For this festival, many airs from this dying tradition were taken down for the first time and published. The society sought premises, having met in various taverns and houses, and in 1802 accepted the offer of a room in the White Linen Hall – from which the modern name of the society's library, the Linen Hall Library, comes.

The society also involved itself in developing a museum. The Belfast Natural History Society (later the Belfast Natural History and Philosophical Society, sometimes known by the acronym BNHPS), founded in 1821, first organised subscriptions for the erection of a museum to house some of the collections of its founding members. These included Sir James Emerson Tennent, the Liberal MP, Reverend Dr Edward Hincks, Assyriologist and antiquarian, rector of Killyleagh, Robert Patterson, naturalist and uncle of Robert Lloyd Praeger and James Shipboy MacAdam, owner of the Soho Foundry. Thomas Duff of Newry and Thomas Jackson, the Quaker architect of St Malachy's Catholic Church in Alfred Street, designed what is now called the Old Museum Building in College Square North (Figure 4.2). In 1833 the

Figure 4.2 Old Museum Building from *Dublin Penny Journal*

Figure 4.3 Linen Hall Library

Dublin Penny Journal wrote that 'There is not perhaps any public institution in Ireland, more interesting in its origin, or honourable to its members and patrons.'[26] Lectures were held and the collections themselves were on show to the members of the public under supervision. They were donated to the Ulster Museum in the early twentieth century, with books and manuscripts going to the Linen Hall Library and Belfast Central Library. The BNHPS still exists, running an annual series of lectures and a publications programme. With the demolition of the White Linen Hall to make way for the Belfast City Hall at the end of the nineteenth century, the Linen Hall Library itself moved across Donegall Square North to a building constructed as a linen warehouse, where it still remains (Figure 4.3).[27]

Organised entertainment of various sorts was also available: a 'concert of vocal and instrumental musick' was advertised at the Boot opposite the Assembly Rooms in 1750;[28] a play, *Mourning bride*, presumably by Congreve, was performed at the Vaults in 1753, followed a few weeks later by a 'tragedy (alter'd from Shakespear) called *Romeo and Juliet*, as it was performed twenty nights successfully at the Theatre Royal in London'.[29] *Hamlet* was performed in 1766.[30] A full-scale music festival, which received the 'unqualified sanction of the public', was held for the first time in 1813.[31] Later, the options for organised entertainment were increased by the opening of the Music Hall in 1840. Tickets to the grand opening concert were priced at a steep six shillings.[32] The 'celebrated pianist Monsieur Liszt' played there in 1841.[33]

Pleasures were to be had outside the town. The *Belfast News Letter* described a holiday scene on Cave Hill in April 1821, with townspeople 'climbing, dancing, racing, tumbling, courting, egg-trundling, frisking [and] laughing'.[34] Seventy years later William Topping recorded the 'simple pleasures' of a late-Victorian childhood with an annual Sunday-school day trip to Newcastle or Whitehead and an Easter-Monday treat at Bellvue Gardens, Glengormley with hobby horses, switchbacks and swings.[35]

There was also, of course, an element of *schadenfreude* in the life of Belfast. The *Belfast News Letter* in the early nineteenth century took a mawkish interest in lurid tales of deaths, murders and assorted mayhem. One was of a drowning in a small stream less than two feet deep: it appeared that 'the unfortunate man had been in Smithfield Market, got intoxicated and had fallen in to the river while driving home an unruly cow'.[36] The activities of resurrectionists were always newsworthy. The abandoned corpse of a tobacco-pipe maker was found in a bag on the Lisburn Road in 1822.[37] Several bodies, including that of a shoemaker's wife, were found in sawdust the next year. These were bound for Edinburgh, calling to mind Burke and Hare, who committed their murders to provide corpses for anatomical study there a few years later.[38] Another four bodies bound for Scotland were found in a piano case in 1829;[39] a man was discovered to have a body in a box on the Dublin Road in 1830. The newspaper delighted to detail that this crime was

Figure 4.4 Coffin cage, Clifton House

discovered by the smell emanating from his luggage.[40] Clifton House still displays a coffin cage, designed to be bolted around the coffin of a fresh corpse to stop the body being stolen (Figure 4.4).

As well as entertaining their readers, newspapers would engage in campaigns for social control – for example, against 'bullet throwing', the traditional pursuit of hurling metal balls along streets, which was banned in 1821 as it caused obstruction,[41] although it was still being played in 1825.[42] More serious matters were also raised when the *Belfast News Letter* declared in 1821 that one cause of vice was:

> the great and unnecessary number of public houses, some of them kept open by persons of very bad character: they were generally kept open the greater part of the night and there the depraved found a refuge from justice and there they deposited their ill-gotten property.[43]

A generation later, Reverend William O'Hanlon ascribed some of the social evils he identified in working-class areas of Belfast to the ready availability of alcohol. In the Talbot Street area:

> 'spirit stores' … meet you at every turn … some of them most imposing looking establishments – and all of them driving a brisk and profitable trade in the material of ruin … One of them … boasts, in its public placards, that it sold, during the first four months of the present year [1853] 9,380 gallons of whiskey alone! Let us think of the fatal effects of such a deluge as this through the households of the poor and we shall cease to wonder at the social degradation and vice that prevail.[44]

O'Hanlon's cry was, 'Cannot and will not the arm of the law interfere to suppress these sources of social ruin – of moral degradation?'[45] At the end of his book, when he moved into policy suggestions, he devoted several pages to a plea for temperance, even prohibition. 'Who will question the dire necessity which exists for such reform in the community,' he asserted, given the links between crime and 'the stimulus of strong drink'? He went on:

> If we could banish alcoholic liquors from common use, placing them among the labelled drugs of the Pharmacopolist, … we should reduce the public crime of the land to a small and inconsiderable fraction of its current amount.[46]

The 'well-regulated comforts' of the Poor House

Alcohol was never banned, but Belfast has a long history of taking other actions to alleviate poverty and encourage social reform. In 1756, at a meeting in the Market House of the sovereign, burgesses and clergy, twenty gentlemen were appointed to form a board. Belfast was to be divided into ten districts, each overseen by two board members. The districts would be inspected and their inhabitants classified into those who could contribute to charity, those who could support themselves and those who required charity, this last group subdivided into different classes depending on their income. Charity payments were to be collected and distributed. A public meeting at the Market House later approved the plan.[47] Poor-relief schemes were subject to renewal – thus in 1766, at a 'season of scarcity and dearth', the sovereign called the town's gentlemen to a meeting at the Market House to consider poor relief again. Here the plans of 1757 and 1758 were considered, approved and readopted.[48] Practical advice on diet was also given at this time:

> To the poor: one pound of rice and two quarts of milk boiled thick as a stirabout, sweetened with two ounces of molasses will make two pounds of good, wholesome food ... and is the best preventative against fluxes and agues, which disorders generally follow a scarcity of bread.[49]

In 1774 a petition was drawn up to beg for relief from the government.[50] 'Public kitchens', as soup kitchens were then called, were opened on occasion. One erected in Smithfield disbursed a quart of soup and a pennyworth of bread to 233 poor people on its first day at Christmas 1799; a few weeks later it was reported that precisely 3,418 shares of bread and broth had been handed out free of charge in the previous week.[51] Detailed arrangements as to the division of Belfast into eleven districts, in each of which collectors would operate to raise money for the public kitchens, were published in July 1800.[52] Other initiatives involved charitable groups: 'young ladies of the town' were selling clothes for the benefit of the poor in Skippers Lane in 1799; the Society for the Employment and Relief of the Poor was set up in 1809.[53]

Some poor people fell into the 'strolling beggars and vagrants' category and did not always receive sympathy and relief. An advertisement in 1757 for a bellhour or beadle made it clear that his duties would be to 'keep the town clear' of such people.[54] In addition to domestic or street support (or expulsion) there was a need for institutions to receive people who could not cope without residential care. One group was those who were mentally ill; it was realised as early as 1771 that such people needed an institution. 'There should be a bedlam in every county … to support their idiots and lunaticks' was how this was phrased in those less politically correct days.[55] In 1821 the sovereign received permission to construct what was then known as the lunatic asylum and sought for a plot of four to six acres with water and a 'gentle proclivity' to assist drainage,[56] although five years later the architect was still looking for a suitable site.[57] Finally, Stevenson's farm on the Falls Road was selected; then there was a six-month delay before a call went out for architects.[58] The first stone was laid in May 1827, and Belfast Lunatic Asylum opened in 1829.[59] Its site was reused for the Royal Victoria Hospital (see Figure 1.3).

Residential care for other categories of people such as the elderly and destitute again fell to private charity – certainly before 1838, when Ireland finally achieved a legislative framework for poor relief, something England had had since the seventeenth century. Even then the system was flawed, banning outdoor relief except in the worst days of the famine. The *Belfast News Letter* had reported upon the town's need for a poor house and a hospital in 1753,[60] at a meeting to which the Belfast Charitable Society dated its foundation. By 1768 this society had collected £1,614 2s 4½d, which 'should be applied to the building of a Poor House and Hospital, agreeable to the original intention of the Scheme, on such ground as Lord Donegall shall be pleased to grant for that purpose'. Such a grant was made at a yearly rent of £9 1s.[61] In 1771 the Belfast Charitable Society, 'having unanimously agreed upon a plan for the intended Poor House and Infirmary … resolved to proceed as far as possible this season in the execution of same' and advertised for someone to supervise the building and later for masons.[62] The town's sovereign, Stewart Banks, laid the foundation stone in August that year.[63] The Poor House, which still exists as Clifton House (Figure 4.5), was built between 1771 and 1774 to a design by an amateur architect, paper-mill owner and newspaper publisher Robert Joy, who served on the board of the society.[64]

Figure 4.5 Clifton House (the Poor House)

A general meeting of the principal householders of Belfast was called in January 1775 to draw up a list of potential inmates. Some could be received at once; others would have to wait until the building was fully finished. The Belfast Charitable Society issued those who were to wait with badges, which licensed them to beg until they could be accommodated.[65] Advertisements for teachers were issued in March 1776,[66] for children of 'whatever religion, and wherever born, are received into the house as scholars where they are boarded and at a proper age bound apprentices to useful trades'.[67] Jonathan Bardon wrote that the 'life chances for these Poor House children were vastly better than for those of cottiers and labourers renting scraps of land' elsewhere in Ulster.[68] The children of strolling beggars were not to be educated in the Poor House – they would be sent to the Foundling Hospital in Dublin, whilst their parents and other 'vagrant beggars who infest the streets were taken to a place of confinement at the Poor House and fed on bread and water'.[69] Begging remained the subject of newspaper complaints[70] and there were further attempts to manage beggars – another badge scheme in 1804, for example. Those not so licensed were apprehended. The *Belfast News Letter* recorded that members of the Charitable Society Committee, 'to free [the public] from the host of beggars who daily besiege their doors' themselves took a black cart round Belfast to seize mendicants and take them to the Poor House. The efficacy of the cart was applauded, for 'the very sight of it gave vigour to the infirm and the lame became so fleet that their most ardent pursuers were completely distanced'.[71] Sir Jerome Fitzpatrick, inspector of jails and infirmaries in Ireland, made an official visit to the Poor House in 1787. He made recommendations regarding both health and economy. One was to move the inmates from 'the underground story' to better-ventilated higher rooms.[72]

The valuable role the Belfast Charitable Society played in the town can be seen by the fact that in the summer of 1783 a hundred aged poor and fifty children were in residential care, 'besides nearly 600 poor housekeepers [perhaps in both senses] who continue to be supplied each fortnight ... according to their various necessities'.[73] No wonder the society was in frequent need of funds, even though 'economy was exercised for feeding and clothing the poor'.[74] A charity sermon was preached at the new St Anne's Parish Church just a few days after it opened in 1776 to raise funds for the Poor House.[75] In 1797 it was admitted that the treasurer of the Poor House was 'in advance' – that is, had spent future income – to the substantial sum of £3,170.[76] Maybe it was not coincidental that a few weeks later the Poor House was left a bequest of £3,200 in the will of prominent businessman Waddell Cunningham, who had made his fortune in trade with the American colonies.[77] However, in 1809 the Belfast Charitable Society had to issue an appeal to the citizens of Belfast as 'the number of old people and children whom they could not refuse to admit ... is considerably greater than at any other period'. Funds were exhausted: 'circumstances so truly embarrassing'.[78] A few years later admissions were suspended for want of funds;[79] but in 1817 the Poor House had 430 inmates, about 130 over its usual number and beyond any comfortable capacity of the buildings as well as the finances.[80] This was a time of fever in the town and the Belfast Charitable Society issued 454 coffins free of charge between 1817 and 1818.[81]

Despite its worthy aims, support from the wealthy classes and town authorities and demands that placed pressure on space and resources, the Poor House did not always find ready acceptance amongst those groups that might have been expected to find its services of value. In common with the House of Industry (and, later, the workhouse), 'an almost insurmountable prejudice' existed against the Poor House: one comment from 1810 stated:

> there is scarce one of the poorest, most friendless outcasts, who would not prefer pining, nay in some instances even perishing in a miserable hovel, to enjoying the cleanly, well regulated comforts of that excellent establishment.[82]

The term 'comforts' may have been optimistic, given the report that the 350 inmates in February 1824 had been served their 'one good meal of the year' to celebrate the earl of Belfast's birthday.[83] With the opening of Belfast Workhouse in 1841, 'the charge of the poor was partly relieved from this ancient establishment'.[84] The Poor House continued; indeed, it was extended in the 1860s and 1870s, with new wings added by benefactors. It continued to care for children until 1882 and the Belfast Charitable Society remains involved in the care of the elderly.[85]

'Great and happy change' in the House of Industry

The establishment of the House of Industry in Smithfield in 1809 was 'an experiment hitherto untried in Ireland'.[86] Eight years earlier the charities running the Poor House, the Fever Hospital and the public kitchens had jointly 'observed certain defects attending their efforts for relief' and recommended the establishment of a public workhouse – the House of Industry.[87] A committee was formed and researched into the operation of such institutions elsewhere in the British Isles, including the type of work carried out by the inmates. They also looked into finding a site, although there was a suggestion that the Poor House itself might be utilised, with up to eight rooms made available. Acting also as a house of industry, with its elements of confinement, labour, and self-improvement, would not have been a completely new departure for the Poor House. Since its inception, it had, as Benn put it, 'preserved ... old and young, the former from want and misery, the latter from idleness and vice'.[88] Recall the bread-and-water diet fed to confined vagrant beggars mentioned above. And, of course, that cotton manufacture was started here is evidence that the inmates were put to work. However, the mission of the new institution was to have a harder edge: to 'confine sturdy vagrants to hard labour'.[89] In the event, a new building, described as 'inconsiderable' by Benn, was erected in 1809.[90] The authorities aimed to:

> assess the number and actual circumstances of the professed beggars who had so long infested the street, to procure a place for their reception, and to supply them with work.[91]

The responsible committee noted, perhaps not wryly, that the number of beggars 'experienced a surprising decrease' as soon as the institution opened – 'many fled from the town, preferring a life of vagrant indolence abroad to one of honest industry at home'. Furthermore:

> many persons ... use every art to return to their former occupation, and ... endeavour to excite prejudice against the Institution by which they are enabled to maintain themselves in comparative comfort.[92]

The public was assured that any tales of distress they heard from inmates were 'fictitious' and they were urged not to give 'private relief'. The House of Industry might be relied upon to impress on its clients 'fixed principals [sic] of sound vital morality', leading, it seemed inevitably, to 'a great and happy change' in them. The change would be brought about by exposing the inmates to the discipline of regular work. The work provided was cotton weaving, flax spinning using wheels and reels or, for those not up to such work, picking oakum. This was a task hard on the hands, consisting as it did of unravelling sections of old ships' rope into their individual fibres. These would be sold on to the navy or shipbuilders, to be stuffed into the gaps between planks and coated with tar, a process known as caulking.

The House of Industry was reserved for the able; those incapable through age or disease were sent to the Poor House; the sick went to the hospitals.[93] The *Belfast News Letter* editorialised:

> We are happy to find that from the exertions of the gentlemen who have undertaken the management of the New Workhouse [i.e. the House of Industry], the streets are completely freed from the strolling vagrants who heretofore infested them … In order to extend relief to a great number of objects, a quantity of soup … is daily provided.[94]

However, by the end of 1810 the House of Industry was in debt and had had to reduce rations to save money,[95] leading the newspaper to wonder if its system was too expensive and whether building it had been wise.[96] This seemed to be the view also of the House of Industry's own committee, which declared debts of over £150 by March 1811 and stated that the 'objects primarily intended to be embraced by this institution … are quite too extensive to be satisfactorily accomplished by the funds entrusted to their management'.[97] Nonetheless, the local authorities continued to send work their way. A few months later the sovereign declared that 'all vagrants and mendicants found on the streets of Belfast will be taken up and kept in close confinement in a place prepared for that purpose … at the House of Industry, Smithfield'.[98] A constable was appointed to apprehend beggars and take them there in 1813, in the traditional black cart.[99] That he was successful might be seen from an 1815 report from a traveller who found Belfast people free from sores and vermin and the streets 'free from the importunities of beggars'.[100] In addition to providing for its inmates, the House of Industry provided domestic work – spinning for females, especially – which George Benn asserted 'obviates that repugnance which many feel at being objects of charity'.[101] In 1817 the House of Industry was supporting above 1,200 families at a cost of £5,000 *per annum*.[102] It had to close for a little while in 1818.[103] Donations were sought; in 1820 the proprietors of the White Linen Hall offered funding, being in favour of paupers being made to work, as was the situation in London and Edinburgh.[104] Later that year the

House of Industry's treasurer received twelve shillings and sixpence from fines levied on four people who were apprehended for the crime of selling potatoes in the street without a licence.[105] Samuel Lewis's *Topographical dictionary of Ireland* of 1837 praised the work of the House of Industry, which had 'diffused great benefit over the town, in which it has entirely abolished mendacity'.[106] However, the institution was threatened with closure once more in February 1841;[107] by June its funds were nearly exhausted and closure within a few days was inevitable.[108] Its functions were taken over by the new Belfast Union Workhouse.

The House of Industry should not be confused with the House of Correction. This had been called for in 1810 as convicted prisoners often escaped custody.[109] A temporary prison, the Black Hole, was built next to the House of Industry in Smithfield in 1812.[110] This accommodated women, but there was still a demand for a House of Correction for Belfast's 'dissipated females',[111] which later transmuted into a demand for a women's penitentiary.[112] The House of Correction itself was designed in 1815 for fifty to sixty prisoners and opened in 1817.[113] It was the only house in Ireland with hard labour in full

Figure 4.6 Belfast Courthouse, Crumlin Road

Figure 4.7 Royal Belfast Academical Institution

operation, the local newspaper had reported with satisfaction in 1825.[114] Its prisoners broke stones for the streets of the town, reported Lewis.[115] Benn mentioned spinning, picking oakum and chopping wood and commented on the salutary effect of its 'strict and correct' discipline in this 'dark, strong building of brick'.[116] The House of Correction also accommodated a courtroom. It soon proved inadequate and by 1840 discussions were taking place about a new jail.[117] This was designed by the omnipresent Charles Lanyon and built for £4,330 on an 8-acre (3.2-hectare) site on the Crumlin Road between 1843 and 1845. When it was built the jail could house 300 prisoners. It was later connected to the 1853 Belfast Courthouse, also designed by Lanyon (Figure 4.6), by a tunnel under Crumlin Road. The old House of Correction's site was still being used as a courthouse in 1844,[118] before being demolished in 1851.

'Struggling to keep out of the Union Workhouse'

Belfast Union Workhouse was opened in 1841 on the Lisburn Road. It was a product of the Irish Poor Law legislation of 1838, in which the country was divided into Poor Law unions, consisting of groups of parishes. The unions had to provide workhouses financed by rates imposed on property owners, which was somewhat resented by many of this class of people in Belfast.[119] Outdoor relief was not part of the role of the workhouse and at the same period a privately funded night asylum was opened in Poultry Square in 1841 to provide at least a space on a floor and a fire for those in need of its scant comforts. A day asylum opened in 1847 at the height of the famine.[120] The workhouses instead used their publicly-provided funds on inmates: in 1841 the Belfast Union Workhouse had 599 inmates; the next year it had 853, of whom 269 were Church of Ireland, 249 Presbyterian, 317 Catholic and 18 of unknown religion 'in consequence of idiocy'.[121] A new master was wanted in 1842 at £50 *per annum* – a respectable rate, given that an apartment, coals, candles and provisions were thrown in. A schoolmaster would receive £30, a schoolmistress £20.[122] The workhouse was the last resort for the poor: 'going up the Lisburn Road' denoted shame and degradation.

There was an infirmary at the workhouse, which was used as a fever hospital in the cholera outbreak of the late 1840s, but it is notable that even *in extremis* the shame attached to being in the workhouse led to a system whereby cholera patients who could afford it might pay for treatment in the General Hospital instead. Anthony McIntyre asked one poor couple why they had not gone to the workhouse and was told by the wife that 'the old man is dying and we like to be together and get to dying in peace'. Another sick woman, who lived in a 'low garret' without furniture, was lying on a pile of rags when McIntyre visited. He recommended that she go into the workhouse as there seemed no other chance of her getting better. The woman 'wept bitterly' at the thought, especially as this would mean separation from her family.[123] McIntyre in general supported people's attempts to stay out of the workhouse. He recommended that his mission obtain a boiler and make up broth to try and relieve their poor families, despite the expense:

> The necessity of such relief as a sort of intermediate charity affording partial aid to a few poor families who are struggling to keep out of the Union Workhouse has been forced on my attention for a length of time. I have seen some of the scholars [at the mission school] pass into the grave, I believe, for want of food.[124]

Although most wished to stay out of it, there were circumstances where entry to the workhouse was better than life outside and admission had to be controlled. McIntyre, as a clergyman, could arrange admittance and he wrote of how he went to the workhouse one morning early in his mission to obtain a copy of the regulations for medical charities and relieving officers; that afternoon he 'gave lines to two poor families to get them admitted'.[125]

'Ignorance abounds': education

One means of social control and advance was to ensure that the population was educated. The topographical information sections of the *Irish historic towns atlas* fascicles show a steady growth in the number of Belfast schools over the period covered in this book.[126] Many of these schools were small and private and must have presented learning of variable quality. By the turn of the eighteenth century there was a demand for a better institution, especially to educate the children of the growing merchant and business classes. This led to the development of the Royal Belfast Academical Institution, now universally known as 'Inst' and still occupying its original premises in the centre of the city (Figure 4.7). Architects were required in 1810 to work under John Soane, the eminent English architect who had earlier designed the Bank of England.[127] The school was opened in February 1814.[128] Other big schools catering largely for a middle-class clientele opened later, including Methodist College (1865), Belfast Royal Academy (1880 in its site on Cliftonville Road, although it was established originally as Belfast Academy in 1785 on Academy Street) and Campbell College (1894).

Figure 4.8 Queen's University Belfast

The Royal Belfast Academical Institution was expected to graduate to university status. However, when the Queen's Colleges were established in the 1840s a different arrangement was made. A new site was chosen for Queen's College Belfast in 1846, on the town side of the already established Botanic Gardens.[129] Designed, again, by Charles Lanyon, the building contract was awarded to Cranston Gregg, the same team responsible for the 1845 Ulster Institute for the Deaf, Dumb and Blind on the Lisburn Road.[130] Queen's College opened in 1849 and became Queen's University Belfast under the Irish Universities Act of 1908 (Figure 4.8).

Students from a social background that would not see them gain ready admittance to Inst or the others, never mind to Queen's, attended different institutions – including those organised on Lancasterian principles, where older pupils, as monitors, taught younger ones. The school on Frederick Street opened in 1811; another in Brown Street, capable of accommodating 500 students, opened in 1814.[131] Other students attended the national schools, many of which were opened after the system started in 1831. However, in 1853 O'Hanlon found that 'an immense mass of the youthful lower

Figure 4.9 Memorial to unmarked burials, Clifton Street Cemetery

population of Belfast is destitute of any means of education'. Although some provision existed, 'ignorance abounds, the schools are generally by no means full, and great irregularity exists as to the character of attendance'.[132]

'Gentlemen and fellow townsmen, the cholera is approaching': health care

Belfast people were subject to epidemic diseases and fevers of various sorts. The General Dispensary of 1792 opened as a charitable venture specifically to 'control the ravages of smallpox by the inoculation of the poor' as well as to relieve the sick poor.[133] The Fever Hospital, opened in 1797 in a series of houses in Factory Row and then West Street,[134] was usually busy: for the period between 1 December 1799 and 1 August 1800, 105 patients were admitted, of whom six died, and 150 fever patients were attended at home, of whom fifteen died. Another 270 people with complaints not connected with fever attended the hospital's dispensary and were treated free of charge.

Running such an operation from a series of houses was obviously unsatisfactory. With some support from the local grand jury and various bequests and donations – including that of the necessary plot of land from the marquis of Donegall – the new Belfast General and Fever Hospital in Frederick Street was begun in 1810.[135] In 1815 the Committee of the Belfast Hospital and Dispensary was 'ready to receive proposals' from architects; the building opened in 1817.[136] It was planned for the new hospital to reserve only thirty of its one hundred beds for fever cases but this ratio would have to be abandoned when epidemics struck.

Cholera, smallpox and typhus were recognised at the time and feared greatly. Newspaper reports would perhaps sensationalise the situation: one report from 1826 declared, 'So prevalent is the cholera morbus in the town that we have heard an instance of one employer who has ten workmen, five of whom are dangerously afflicted with the complaint.'[137] Six years later, however, fears of a major outbreak – 'Gentlemen and fellow townsmen, the cholera is approaching'[138] – did come true. The severity of the 1832 outbreak overwhelmed the General and Fever Hospital itself, which was too small and in debt (an appeal had had to be launched).[139] Many patients had to be accommodated in other institutions: premises in Millfield, Dublin Road and at the rear of the existing fever hospital were established.[140] It was assumed that the approach of the cholera would be from Scotland and there were calls to restrict passage through Donaghadee and to ban the receipt of parcels of old clothes.[141] The *Belfast News Letter* reported in March that a lighterman had brought the disease into his property in the poor district of Johnny's Entry off Talbot Street and three of the four members of his household had died.[142] Nonetheless, there was a confident assertion a week later that Belfast was free from cholera.[143] This was premature, for in April the disease reappeared, with six cases reported in ten days, again in the poor districts – Coar's Lane was mentioned.[144] By early June there had been seventeen cases with fourteen fatalities;[145] by late September there had been 2,588 cases and 357 deaths,[146] 73 of which, according to J.S. Logan, were in the General and Fever Hospital.[147] Both Friar's Bush and Clifton Street Cemeteries were used for burials – common, anonymous burials in cholera pits, although, in the words of the memorial to people buried without markers in Clifton Street cemetery, 'they all had names' (Figure 4.9). The cholera pit in Friar's Bush formed a mound called Plaguey Hill, which was reopened in 1847 for victims of typhus.[148] One Dr Thompson published his treatment for cholera in 1832, which seems almost as unpleasant as the disease:

> I order a pint of arrowroot, a glass and a half of whiskey, 80 or 100 drops of laudanum, all to be mixed together and made sufficiently thin for an enema, and to be thrown up the intestines as warm as the patient can bear it. [Some patients] suffered to such an alarming degree that I was frequently attacked.[149]

The General and Fever Hospital was unable to cope with another outbreak of cholera in 1840, when its then 123 beds were overwhelmed by 182 patients; a town meeting was called to discuss the situation.[150] Money that was to have been spent on illuminating the town in celebration of Queen Victoria's wedding was instead donated to the hospital. No one would have understood the reason for this 'better than the Queen herself', it was asserted.[151] Typhus soon followed, although it was later suggested that some patients had the milder disease of trench fever instead.[152] At one time there were 450 patients in the hospital at the newly opened Belfast Union Workhouse and another 50 in the General and Fever Hospital.[153] In the later 1840s Belfast was affected to some extent by the Irish famine: 'this town is in a state of destitution more appalling than is commonly believed', wrote the Belfast General Relief Fund,[154] and its citizens were ill able to withstand further epidemics such as the typhus outbreak in 1847. It was thought that typhus spread amongst the people through the day and night asylums, refuges provided for the homeless who had come into Belfast. Medical and surgical patients had to be evacuated from the General and Fever Hospital to the Poor House in order to allow the hospital to focus on fever. Sheds were erected in the grounds to create room for 600 fever patients.[155] The old military barracks in Barrack Street was also pressed into service, especially for patients who could be moved there from the night asylum.[156] By June the accommodation in the workhouse, Frederick Street and Barrack Street totalled 1,300 beds, but this still left 1,200 other patients without proper care. Tented encampments had to be erected for these patients.[157] Having been the

Date	Cases	Deaths	Comments
12 September			'the too probable approach of cholera'
15 September			advice to mill workers
22 September			advice to people of Dock Ward
6 October			workhouse fever ward doctor advertised
12 December	1	1	man dies in workhouse
19 December	?	8	in workhouse, including four children
27 December	24	?	dispensary stations in Cromac St and Frederick St
12 January	97	?	several cases in poor parts of town, the rest in the workhouse
30 January	208	?	rapidly progressing
23 February	563	196	
27 February			cases rise after 'fatal dissipation' of 'lower classes over the weekend'
20 March			on the decline
18 May	1,745	515	
12 June			still not gone from the town
15 June	2,016	594	
20 July			'invaded the more affluent class', who could pay for treatment outside the workhouse, in the General Hospital; not wholly confined to [the poor district of] Cromac
10 August			on the decline; latest victim was a dentist

Source: *Belfast News Letter*.

Table 4.1. Cholera in Belfast, 1848–9.

focus of the 'desolating epidemic which is now raging in our town', the night asylum was closed down in July and steps were taken 'to send all strangers to their proper place of settlement'.[158]

It was feared that cholera would return in 1848. The public bath-houses and washrooms were prepared, whilst meetings were held in mills to advise the operatives on ways to avoid the disease. The authorities were right to be worried, as Table 4.1 demonstrates.

In 1849 all fever patients were treated at the workhouse site. The General and Fever Hospital (retitled the Belfast Royal Hospital in

1875) focused on other health matters. By the turn of the century the hospital, built in 1817, had become too small and its accommodation and facilities were below par for a city of Belfast's size. It was replaced by the new Royal Victoria Hospital, built on the grounds of the Belfast Asylum on the Grosvenor Road in 1903. Harland and Wolff partner Sir William Pirrie was one of the principal movers and benefactors of the new hospital, which was opened by Edward VII and Queen Alexandra. The Mater Infirmorum opened on Crumlin Road in 1883. It was a foundation of the Sisters of Mercy, although it accepted patients of any creed. In 1908 it joined the Royal Victoria Hospital in the instruction of medical students from Queen's University as part of the Belfast Medical School.[159]

Meanwhile, the Union Workhouse was dealing with fever patients. In 1853 William O'Hanlon described once more 'the fever car ... bearing away to hospital some wretched victim of miasma and foulness'.[160] At the same period, Anthony McIntyre was told of several deaths from cholera:

> three young women, all very fine looking girls, said Mrs McCoy, died out of one house there (pointing to it) last week. One of them had been in a house in Kittle's Entry ... and had washed the feet of a person that had cholera. She came home, took ill and died the next day ... [the] two other women had been taken to the Cholera Hospital and have both died.[161]

McIntyre wondered at the lack of action by the medical authorities to clean out the houses of victims:

> On calling to visit Woods, No 3 Stephens Street, they informed me that a woman had died out of the house they live in of cholera about a fortnight before, and that the apartments had never been cleaned out since. That it was all remaining as she had been taken out ... I enquired if they had not made application to the Sanitary Committee to have the apartments cleaned out. I was told they had two or three times.[162]

McIntyre took this matter up himself with the Police Committee and it was 'attended to immediately'.[163] O'Hanlon also made a plea for money to be spent on prevention, 'proverbially easier than cure'.[164] The message eventually got through and Councillor O'Neill wrote in 1901 of how the poor conditions in Belfast had helped to lead to the 'great series of Public Health Acts, and from 1849 to 1899 there has scarcely been a session of parliament in which measures relating to public health have not been passed, becoming more stringent every year'.[165]

'Dissolute females' and 'respectable ladies'

Belfast was unusual in that its range of industries provided productive work for both genders. Prior to the factory system, traditional roles were seen – women were treated as property. A linen weaver put a notice in the newspaper in 1757, for example, seeking news of his eloped wife.[166] Changes occurred with industrialisation in that many women were able to take on their own jobs outside the home. Gender differences were evident – the engineering and shipbuilding trades were dominated by men, whilst most working-class women were employed in certain sectors of the linen industry. As we have seen, women's work in the mills was generally hard, unhealthy and ill rewarded but it gave them a role away from the family, which denoted a status and independence not always available elsewhere. That such was needed might be evinced by the comment of one woman sentenced to be transported in 1827 for stealing two sacks. She thanked the court, remarking that transportation was better than a bad marriage.[167] There was a cultural and social turn from women's work, which can be identified, for example, from Betty Messenger's study of the folklore of the linen business as revealed by interviews she carried out with people who had worked in the industry in the early twentieth century.[168]

The fact that many women had opportunities for regular employment did not necessarily bring social quietude to Belfast's streets. In 1813 the town reportedly, was troubled by 'dissolute females who daily perambulate our streets [and who] ought immediately to be taken up ... their nightly brawls disturb the inhabitants in almost every part of the town'.[169] By 1816 the streets were 'no longer infested by those dissolute females, who were so offensive to decency and good morals',[170] but this state did not last – by 1820 'the number of disorderly females who infest our streets has increased [sic], is encreasing and ought to be diminished'. So wrote one 'Simon Pure', presumably a fictitious name, when calling for a review of prostitution.[171] Some idea as to the scale of the problem can be see from a report that forty-seven women were apprehended for 'being disorderly on the street' one summer night in 1822.[172] There were also reports of brothels, one in Francis Street in 1821, another in Blue Bell Entry in 1822. The (male) brothel owner was named in both cases.[173] The women worked outdoors, too – a prostitute died, presumably through exposure, when left to the elements in the winter of 1825.[174] In the following year came a report that:

> the mouths of the different entries as well as the more open parts of
> the streets were literally swarming with drunken men, chiefly sailors,
> and unfortunate women on the watch for their pray [sic].[175]

Some of the women were really only girls. One report spoke of them being as young as twelve and identified a 'need for planting little [Sunday] schools in the lanes and alleys' to direct the children onto a better path.[176]

Some women also begged. One was prosecuted in 1840, having borrowed the body of another woman's dead child in order to increase her chances of success as a beggar.[177] William O'Hanlon drew attention to prostitution and other social 'ulcers' in 1853. He ascribed much of the cause to poor and overcrowded housing conditions, with:

> Families all occupying the same room – fathers, mothers, brothers
> and sisters all sleeping indiscriminately upon the floor … How can
> a particle of self-respect or any sense of the becoming live in such a
> region, and amid such circumstances? All the safeguards of morality
> are thrown down, and a coarse brutality produced, forming the rank
> and fertile seed plot for every imaginable vice and crime. If incest,
> that most loathsome of all the ulcers that have ever appeared in the
> social body be avoided, (and who can hope that it is?) the descent
> from such a state of domestic life to the degradation of the street
> walker and the prostitute is so easy and natural, that we may cease
> to wonder at the number of those forlorn wretches who swarm in our
> alleys and lanes at night, or at the number of houses of ill-fame to be
> found in the lower streets of our town.[178]

He mentioned where several such institutions were to be found: a court off Barrack Street where of the nine houses, seven were 'abodes of guilt'. 'Passers of base coin' and thieves shared this district. One crime was to lure sailors from the docks 'like unwary birds' allured 'into these pitfalls, where they are soon peeled and plundered'.[179] Similarly, in Round Entry, where the brothels were termed 'bawdy houses':

> unwary youth are entrapped and drawn into these places as flies into a spider's web – inebriated, robbed, and then turned out guilty, ruined, stricken, with a sting in their conscience and a stain upon their character.[180]

O'Hanlon, whose stern views on matters of morality led him into rhetorical flourishes, than assumed such youths would inevitably 'plunge headlong [into a] career of vice and degradation'.[181] In cases where there might be also outcomes of a medical nature, there was the confidence of the assertion from Hodges, a pharmacist in High Street, that there was available a 'lignum' with the use of which men might cure themselves of venereal disease.[182]

O'Hanlon's observations convinced him that there was still much to be done to relieve women from the 'territories of loathsomeness':[183]

> Can no mission of mercy be formed to visit the haunts of these fallen and wretched ones and to draw them out of the pit in which they have sunk? Would it be Utopian to expect that among the benevolent, the high-minded and Christian women of Belfast; some few at least might be found who, striking out of the beaten path, would dare to be singularly great in their mode of doing good[?][184]

Once drawn out of the pit, there were some places where the fallen ones could go. One was the Ulster Female Penitentiary, which had opened in York Lane in 1820 with twelve residential places and a programme of work after 'a number of respectable ladies' had established a subscription list.[185] Thanks to the efforts of a Presbyterian minister, Reverend John Edgar, the penitentiary moved to a bigger building in Brunswick Street in 1839.[186] This was capable of accommodating fifty-four women in private rooms and provided them with work in a laundry. O'Hanlon wrote that the penitentiary reflected 'honour upon its originator and friends; and who can calculate the blessings it has conferred upon many a broken-hearted and desolate female[?]'[187] O'Hanlon, indeed, wanted its work extended. Upon his visit only seventeen places were occupied, he felt because the Union Workhouse had diverted some of its potential clients. In 1892, the name was changed to the Edgar Home, as 'penitentiary' was considered to smack of retribution. The premises were moved to Sunnyside Street in 1902 and the laundry operated there until 1924.[188] A second institution was the Ulster Magdalene Asylum, which, together with a chapel, had opened in 1849 on Donegall Pass. By early 1850 it housed twenty penitent females from Belfast and elsewhere in Ulster, although there was dormitory accommodation for fifty.[189] It housed only young women, but they could be of any religion. They had to carry out needlework and labour in the laundry. It closed in 1916; Jordan estimates that during its sixty-seven-year life it had 'given shelter to, maintained, employed, instructed and encouraged upwards of 3000 women of all denominations'.[190] Catholic women – not necessarily (former) prostitutes, but rather those who were abandoned by their families or who found themselves in difficulties such as becoming pregnant out of wedlock – could also be supported at the Good Shepherd Convent on the Ormeau Road, which opened in 1869 and had 140 places. It was remodelled in 1906. It, too, ran a laundry, as was usually the case with such establishments.[191]

There was a long tradition of middle-class Belfast women occupying themselves with charity work. At the end of 1793 it was reported that the 'ladies of Belfast are at present busily engaged in the laudable institution of a lying-in hospital', an institution that would now be termed a maternity hospital.[192] These ladies founded the Humane Female Society for the Relief of Lying-In Women.[193] There was a proud report from the Lying-in Hospital on Donegall Street in 1813 stating that during its nineteen years of existence it had only had to appeal to the public for assistance twice.[194] In 1826 the hospital reported that it had taken in 800 patients in the previous six years but was in need of upgrading. Instead, the old building being considered inadequate, it was replaced. An advertisement for a builder for a new establishment was issued in 1829.[195] In 1849 there were 256 admissions; 258 babies were born and only one mother died. The charity was available only to married women – humanity had its limits, it would seem.[196]

The Belfast Ladies' Clothing Society was founded in 1819 as the Female Society for Clothing the Poor; the Belfast Female Society had a mission to 'relieve the sufferings attendant upon want of the most necessary articles of clothing among the poor of Belfast'.[197] It had relieved 280 families by 1813, by which time it had incurred a debt of £20 and had to cease work.[198] The Female Temperance Society was operating in 1842[199] and the Belfast Ladies' Association for the Relief of Irish Distress was meeting in 1847;[200] at the same time the ladies of the Industrial Relief Committee were seeking orders for shirts, petticoats and other items to be given in to the House of Correction.[201] Anthony McIntyre wrote in 1854 of the 'Destitute Sick Society that is managed by a committee of ladies … all Protestant or rather Presbyterian … the same ladies who formed the committee of the general Clothing Society'.[202] Jonathan Bardon singles out for specific mention Mary Ann McCracken, who had been deeply involved in the 1798 rebellion and who ran a muslin business with her sister. She was 'the driving force behind the Ladies' Committee [of the Poor House] … for almost all of its existence'.[203]

Alison Jordan's book details charitable bodies in Victorian and Edwardian Belfast, including the Ulster Society for Promoting the Education of the Deaf and Dumb and the Blind, other charities for the blind, the Cripples' Institute, the Society for the Encouragement and Reward of Good Conduct of Female Servants, the Society for Providing Nurses for the Sick Poor, the Society for the Relief of the Destitute Sick, the Provident Home, which sheltered newly arrived women, and the Midnight Mission, which offered shelter to women found on the streets late at night. Most of the women involved in these charities were Protestant; Catholics, female and male, tended to work through the Society of St Vincent de Paul, which operated in Belfast from the 1850s and, as with the Good Shepherd Convent, through religious orders. These included the Sisters of Mercy, which opened a convent school and female penitentiary in Hamilton Street in 1854, before moving to the Crumlin Road. Jordan also mentions the Irish branch of the Dominicans, the Bon Secours, the Sisters of Nazareth and the Sisters of Charity.[204]

NOTES

1   *BNL*, 12 May 1772.
2   O'Hanlon, *Walks among the poor*, p. 49.
3   *BNL*, 28 February 1823.
4   Ibid., 13 March 1821.
5   Ibid., 6 September 1816.
6   Ibid., 4 December 1827.
7   Ibid., 12 February 1828.
8   Ibid., 4 June 1839.
9   Ibid., 10 April 1821.
10 Ibid., 15 July 1823.
11 Ibid., 29 November 1822.
12 Ibid., 6 January 1825.
13 Ibid., 25 June 1822.
14 Ibid., 29 November 1822.
15 Ibid., 30 July 1776.
16 Ibid., 29 December 1861.
17 Ibid., 13 August 1773.
18 Ibid., 5 December 1800.
19 Ibid., 25 September 1801.
20 Ibid., 9 November 1802.
21 Ibid., 18 June 1784, 20 July 1784.
22 Ibid., 25 April 1823, 29 April 1823.
23 Ibid., 15 September 1812.
24 Rodgers, *Return room*, p. 50.
25 John Killen, *A history of the Linen Hall Library, 1788–1988* (Belfast, 1990), p. 1.
26 *Dublin Penny Journal*, 19 January 1833.
27 Killen, *Linen Hall Library*.
28 *BNL*, 15 June 1750.
29 Ibid., 5 June 1753.
30 Ibid., 25 February 1766.
31 Ibid., 22 September 1813.
32 Ibid., 6 March 1840, 20 March 1840.
33 Ibid., 8 January 1841.
34 Ibid., 9 April 1822.
35 Topping, Memoirs.
36 *BNL*, 10 April 1821.
37 Ibid., 12 November 1822.
38 Ibid., 25 February 1823.
39 Ibid.
40 Ibid., 9 March 1830.
41 Ibid., 11 September 1821.
42 Ibid., 1 July 1825.
43 Ibid., 18 September 1821.
44 O'Hanlon, *Walks among the poor*, p. 9.
45 Ibid., p. 14.
46 Ibid., pp. 125, 126.
47 *BNL*, 7 December 1756, 14 December 1756, 18 December 1756.

48 Ibid., 14 February 1766, 18 February 1766.
49 Ibid., 1 July 1766.
50 Ibid., 11 January 1774.
51 Ibid., 24 December 1799, 18 February 1800.
52 Ibid., 1 July 1800.
53 Ibid., 24 December 1799, 4 July 1809.
54 Ibid., 11 October 1757.
55 Ibid., 1 October 1771.
56 Ibid., 30 January 1821.
57 Ibid., 12 August 1825.
58 Ibid., 26 May 1826, 7 November 1826.
59 Ibid., 18 May 1827, 26 May 1829.
60 Ibid., 6 July 1753.
61 G.K. Smith and W. Hughes, Chronological statement in reference to the origin and operations of the Belfast Charitable Society (LHL, BPB1879/7).
62 *BNL*, 21 May 1771, 12 July 1771.
63 Ibid., 2 August 1771.
64 Bardon, *Interesting and honourable history*.
65 *BNL*, 13 January 1775, 14 February 1775.
66 Ibid., 26 March 1776.
67 Ibid., 14 August 1792.
68 Bardon, *Interesting and honourable history*, p. 19.
69 *BNL*, 4 December 1778.
70 Ibid., 30 March 1793.
71 Ibid., 24 July 1804.
72 Ibid., 2 October 1787.
73 Ibid., 29 July 1783.
74 Smith and Hughes, Chronological statement.
75 *BNL*, 25 October 1776.
76 Ibid., 13 October 1797.
77 Ibid., 18 December 1797.
78 Ibid., 5 December 1809.
79 Ibid., 2 August 1814.
80 Ibid., 1 April 1817.
81 Ibid., 15 December 1818.
82 Rules and regulations for the House of Industry, Belfast, to be laid before a general meeting of the town for their approbation, 1810 (LHL, BPP32).
83 *BNL*, 10 February 1824.
84 Ibid., 3 December 1841.
85 Bardon, *Interesting and honourable history*.
86 Rules and regulations for the House of Industry.
87 *BNL*, 28 April 1801.
88 Benn, *History of the town of Belfast*, p. 106.
89 *BNL*, 15 May 1801.
90 Benn, *History of the town of Belfast*, p. 107.
91 Rules and regulations for the House of Industry.
92 Ibid.
93 Ibid.
94 *BNL*, 20 October 1809.
95 Ibid., 16 November 1810.
96 Ibid., 8 February 1811.

97 Ibid., 22 March 1811.
98 Ibid., 22 October 1811.
99 Ibid., 2 November 1813, 29 August 1817.
100 Ibid., 12 September 1815.
101 Benn, *History of the town of Belfast*, pp. 107–08.
102 *BNL*, 1 April 1817.
103 Ibid., 17 April 1817, 24 April 1817.
104 Ibid., 1 February 1820.
105 Ibid., 10 October 1820.
106 Lewis, 'Belfast', p. 199.
107 *BNL*, 9 February 1841.
108 Ibid., 4 June 1841.
109 Ibid., 13 November 1810.
110 Ibid., 3 July 1812, 29 September 1812.
111 Ibid., 18 October 1814.
112 Ibid., 27 July 1819.
113 Ibid., 24 March 1814.
114 Ibid., 20 September 1825.
115 Lewis, 'Belfast', pp. 191–201.
116 Benn, *History of the town of Belfast*, p. 108.
117 *BNL*, 4 August 1840.
118 BCM, 1 May 1844 (PRONI, LA/7/2/EA/1).
119 Virginia Crossman, *The Poor Law in Ireland, 1838–1948* (Dundalk, 2006); *BNL*, 23 April 1847; Christine Kinealy and Gerard MacAtasney, *The hidden famine: hunger, poverty and sectarianism in Belfast, 1840–50* (London, 2000).
120 Jordan, *Who cared?*
121 *BNL*, 28 January 1842, 12 July 1842.
122 Ibid., 8 April 1842.
123 McIntyre, Diary (PRONI, D1558/2/3), p. 236.
124 Ibid., p. 315.
125 Ibid., p. 83.
126 Gillespie and Royle, *Belfast, part I: Irish historic towns atlas*; Royle, *Belfast, part II: Irish historic towns atlas*.
127 *BNL*, 20 February 1810.
128 Ibid., 4 February 1814.
129 Ibid., 13 March 1846.
130 Ibid., 2 March 1847.
131 Ibid., 31 August 1810.
132 O'Hanlon, *Walks among the poor*, p. 109.
133 *BNL*, 10 April 1792.
134 R.S. Allison, *The seeds of time: being a short history of the Belfast General and Royal Hospital 1850/1903* (Belfast, 1972).
135 *BNL*, 11 May 1810.
136 Ibid., 14 April 1815.
137 Ibid., 8 September 1826.
138 Ibid., 17 February 1832.
139 Ibid., 16 March 1832.
140 Ibid., 3 February 1832, 7 February 1832, 14 February 1832, 17 February 1832, 21 February 1832.
141 Ibid., 21 February 1832.
142 Ibid., 20 March 1832.

143 Ibid., 27 March 1832.
144 Ibid., 27 April 1832.
145 Ibid., 8 June 1832.
146 Ibid., 28 September 1832.
147 J.S. Logan, 'Trench fever in Belfast, and the nature of the "relapsing fevers" of the United Kingdom in the nineteenth century' in *Ulster Medical Journal*, lviii, no. 1 (1989), pp. 83–8.
148 Phoenix, *Two acres of Irish history*.
149 *BNL*, 28 August 1832.
150 Ibid., 11 February 1840, 27 March 1840.
151 O'Neill, 'Sanitary science', p. 40.
152 Logan, 'Trench fever'.
153 *BNL*, 18 September 1841.
154 Ibid., 23 April 1847. See also Kinealy and MacAtasney, *Hidden famine*.
155 *BNL*, 11 May 1847.
156 Ibid., 25 May 1847.
157 Ibid., 1 June 1847, 4 June 1847, 8 June 1847.
158 Ibid., 27 June 1847.
159 Allison, *Seeds of time*.
160 O'Hanlon, *Walks among the poor*, p. 17.
161 McIntyre, Diary, pp. 188–9.
162 Ibid., pp. 205–06.
163 Ibid., p. 206.
164 O'Hanlon, *Walks among the poor*, p. 17.
165 O'Neill, 'Sanitary science', p. 41.
166 *BNL*, 20 May 1757.
167 Ibid., 14 August 1827.
168 Betty Messenger, *Picking up the linen threads: a study in industrial folklore* (Belfast, 1980).
169 *BNL*, 31 August 1813.
170 Ibid., 11 October 1816.
171 Ibid., 27 October 1820.
172 Ibid., 27 August 1822.
173 Ibid., 21 May 1822, 9 July 1822.
174 Ibid., 18 November 1825.
175 Ibid., 28 April 1826.
176 Ibid., 31 August 1827.
177 Ibid., 21 February 1840.
178 O'Hanlon, *Walks among the poor*, p. 5.
179 Ibid., p. 16.
180 Ibid., p. 22.
181 Ibid.
182 *BNL*, 14 April 1820.
183 O'Hanlon, *Walks among the poor*, p. 97.
184 Ibid.
185 *BNL*, 27 July 1819, 24 August 1819, 27 August 1819, 31 August 1819.
186 Ibid., 26 April 1839.
187 O'Hanlon, *Walks among the poor*, p. 97.
188 Jordan, *Who cared?*
189 *BNL*, 18 January 1850.
190 Jordan, *Who cared?*, p. 178.

191 Ibid.
192 *BNL*, 31 December 1793.
193 Ibid., 29 September 1826.
194 Ibid., 2 June 1815.
195 Ibid., 5 June 1829, 14 July 1829.
196 Ibid., 19 March 1850.
197 *BNL*, 5 February 1813.
198 Ibid.
199 Ibid., 20 May 1842.
200 Ibid., 12 February 1847.
201 Ibid., 19 March 1847.
202 McIntyre, Diary, p. 228.
203 Bardon, *Interesting and honourable history*, p. 32. See also Mary McNeill, *The life and times of Mary Ann McCracken 1770–1866: a Belfast panorama* (Dublin, 1960).
204 Jordan, *Who cared?*

POSTSCRIPT

BELFAST IN 1914:
'REALLY A WONDER'?

The Belfast journalist and novelist Frank Frankfort Moore wrote in 1914, the close of the period considered in this book on Belfast, that:

> Belfast is really a wonder. It has been growing in the past seventy years as few towns in the world have been, but it has not outgrown its strength. It has been well looked after morally as well as physically and the result is that to-day it can do what few other cities can do. It can launch the largest ships that the world has ever seen ... it has the largest rope works in existence, and the largest spinning mill. For the production of such luxuries as whisky and tobacco in marketable form Belfast stands pre-eminent in the Customs list. For a variety of industries, and for every one of them all being a world's record in production, there is no city in the kingdom that can compete with Belfast ... no matter in what direction one goes in Belfast, one is brought face to face with stupendous statistics.[1]

A few years earlier, R.M. Young had also written in his *Old times in Belfast* of 'the wonderful changes which have occurred',[2] whilst the *Irish Ecclesiastical Gazette* had published an article on Belfast's new cathedral being erected to replace the 1770s parish church, which had stated:

> we are very proud of ourselves ... a cathedral ... will be in keeping with our commercial greatness, and being so will of necessity be the finest church in Ireland, even as Belfast is by far the first and foremost of Irish cities.[3]

'Wonder(ful)', 'largest', 'pre-eminent', 'stupendous', 'greatness', 'finest', 'first and foremost': no wonder Belfast was 'proud'. The city was bursting into the twentieth century, powered by its industrial and commercial might. However, its long-standing social and sectarian divisions were intact; furthermore, the loss of the *Titanic* in 1912 came to embody the city's subsequent economic decline. This book ends at 1914, just as the Great War and its aftermath were about to engender significant social and political transformations. Belfast's experience in the rest of the twentieth century was not one that would merit 'wonder' in a positive sense from Frank Frankfort Moore or anyone else. Instead, the 'enduring city' would become associated with sectarianism, violence, poverty and exploitation.[4] As this book has shown, these negative attributes were already to be found behind the façade of the city of 1914, despite Belfast being so 'well looked after'. Indeed, some have said that Belfast, even at the peak of its 'commercial greatness', ought anyway to have tempered that contemporary smugness:

> Every stone [of the] 'dark Satanic mills' of which Belfast boasts ... is cemented by the blood and sweat and tears of ... half-starved and half-naked children, and thus was laid in the beginning the foundation of the fortunes of the 'Linen Lords' which enabled them, on their broad acres to raise in the midst of their woods and gardens, the magnificent and luxurious summer residences with which the city is ringed round, and of which as evidences of 'Belfast's wealth and prosperity', we are all told – and in all seriousness – we should all feel proud.[5]

NOTES

1 Frank Frankfort Moore, *The truth about Ulster* (London, 1914), pp. 277–8.
2 R.M. Young, 'Old times in Belfast' in *Journal of the Royal Society of Antiquaries of Ireland*, xxxv, no. 4 (1905), p. 377.
3 *Irish Ecclesiastical Gazette*, 21 June 1895.
4 Frederick W. Boal and Stephen A. Royle (eds), *Enduring city: Belfast in the twentieth century* (Belfast, 2006).
5 Cathal O'Byrne, *As I roved out: a book of the north, being a series of historical sketches of Ulster and old Belfast* (Belfast, 1946), p. 134.

SELECTED BIBLIOGRAPHY

Books and articles

Allison, R.S., *The seeds of time: being a short history of the Belfast General and Royal Hospital 1850/1903* (Belfast, 1972).

Anon, 'Belfast Tories' in *The London Review* (22 July 1865), p. 82.

—, 'The borough of Belfast' in *The London Review* (1 April 1865), pp. 345–6.

Armstrong, D.L., 'Social and economic conditions in the Belfast linen industry, 1850–1900' in *Irish Historical Studies*, vii, no. 28 (1951), pp. 235–69.

Baker, Sybil E., 'Orange and green: Belfast, 1832–1912' in H.J. Dyos and Michael Wolff (eds), *The Victorian city: images and realities* (London, 1973), ii, pp. 789–814.

Bardon, Jonathan, *An interesting and honourable history: the Belfast Charitable Society, the first 250 years, 1752–2002* (Belfast, 2002).

—, 'Belfast at its zenith' in *History Ireland*, i, no. 4 (winter 1993).

—, *Belfast: an illustrated history* (Belfast, 1982).

Belfast Chamber of Commerce, *Mr Gladstone's speech to the Belfast Chamber of Commerce and the chamber's reply* (Belfast, 1893).

Benn, George, *The history of the town of Belfast* (Belfast, 1823).

Boal, Frederick W. and Royle, Stephen A. (eds), *Enduring city: Belfast in the twentieth century* (Belfast, 2006).

Bulfin, William, *Rambles in Eirinn* (Dublin, 1907).

Callan, P., 'Rambles in Éirinn, by William Bulfin' in *Studies: An Irish Quarterly Review*, lxxi, no. 284 (winter 1982), pp. 391–8.

Calvert, Raymond, 'The ballad of William Bloat' (www.antiromantic.com/ballad-of-william-bloat) (25 August 2011).

Campbell, R. Timothy and Royle, Stephen A., 'East Belfast and the suburbanization of north-west County Down in the nineteenth century' in L.J. Proudfoot (ed.), *Down, history and society: interdisciplinary essays on the history of an Irish county* (Dublin, 1997), pp. 629–62.

Charlotte Elizabeth (Mrs C.E. Tonna), *Letters from Ireland 1837* (London, 1838).

Craig, Patricia (ed.), *The Belfast anthology* (Belfast, 1999).

Crossman, Virginia, *The Poor Law in Ireland, 1838–1948* (Dundalk, 2006).

Douglas, James, *The unpardonable sin* (Belfast, 1907) (cited in Patricia Craig (ed.), *The Belfast anthology* (Belfast, 1999)).

Dubourdieu, John, *A statistical survey of the County of Antrim, with observations on the means of improvement* (Dublin, 1812).

Engels, Friedrich, *The condition of the working class in England* (Leipzig, 1845) (English ed. New York, 1887).

Ewart, Wilfrid H.G., *A journey in Ireland* (London, 1922).

Fagan, Henry Stuart, *Orange Ulster* (London, 1879).

Gillespie, Raymond, *Early Belfast: the origins and growth of an Ulster town to 1750* (Belfast, 2007).

Gillespie, Raymond and Royle, Stephen A., *Belfast, part I, to 1840: Irish historic towns atlas no. 12* (Dublin, 2003).

Gray, John, *City in revolt: James Larkin and the Belfast dock strike of 1907* (Belfast, 1985).

Hartley, Tom, *Written in stone: the history of Belfast City Cemetery* (Belfast, 2006).

Hepburn, Anthony C. and Collins, Brenda, 'Industrial society: the structure of Belfast, 1901' in Peter Roebuck (ed.) *Plantation to partition: essays in Ulster history in honour of J.L. McCracken* (Belfast, 1981), pp. 210–28.

Irvine, Alexander, *My lady of the chimney corner* (New York, 1913).

Jones, Emrys, 'The social geography of Belfast' in *Journal of the Statistical and Social Inquiry Society of Ireland*, xxix, no. 2 (1954).

Jordan, Alison, *Who cared? Charity in Victorian and Edwardian Belfast* (Belfast, 1993).

Killen, John, *A history of the Linen Hall Library, 1788–1988* (Belfast, 1990).

Kinealy, Christine and MacAtasney, Gerard, *The hidden famine: hunger, poverty and sectarianism in Belfast, 1840–50* (London, 2000).

Lewis, Samuel, 'Belfast' in *The topographical dictionary of Ireland* (London, 1837), i.

Logan, J.S., 'Trench fever in Belfast, and the nature of the "relapsing fevers" of the United Kingdom in the nineteenth century' in *Ulster Medical Journal*, lviii, no. 1 (1989), pp. 83–8.

—, 'Flax-dust byssinosis and chronic non-tuberculous chest disease in Belfast' in *Ulster Medical Journal*, xxviii, no. 2 (1959), pp. 164–75.

Loudan, Jack, *In search of water, being a history of the Belfast water supply* (Belfast, 1940).

Maguire, W.A., *Living like a lord: the second marquis of Donegall, 1769–1844* (Belfast, 1984).

—, 'Lord Donegall and the sale of Belfast: a case history from the Encumbered Estates Court' in *Economic History Review*, xxix, no. 4 (1976), pp. 570–84.

Malcolm, Andrew G., 'The influence of factory life on the health of the operative as founded upon the medical statistics of this class at Belfast' in *Journal of the Statistical Society of London*, xix, no. 2 (1856).

—, *The sanitary state of Belfast with suggestions for its improvement* (Belfast, 1852).

McCutcheon, W.A., *The industrial archaeology of Northern Ireland* (Belfast, 1980).

McNeill, Mary, *The life and times of Mary Ann McCracken 1770–1866: a Belfast panorama* (Dublin, 1960).

Messenger, Betty, *Picking up the linen threads: a study in industrial folklore* (Belfast, 1980).

Monaghan, John J., 'The rise and fall of the Belfast cotton industry' in *Irish Historical Studies*, iii, no. 9 (1942), pp. 1–17.

Moore, Frank Frankfort, *The truth about Ulster* (London, 1914).

Moore, John, 'On the influence of flax spinning on the health of the mill workers of Belfast' in *Transactions of the National Association for the Promotion of Social Science: Belfast meeting 1867* (London, 1868 (also LHL, N13668)).

Moss, Michael and Hume, John R., *Shipbuilders to the world: 125 years of Harland and Wolff, Belfast 1861–1986* (Belfast, 1986).

O'Byrne, Cathal, *As I roved out: a book of the north, being a series of historical sketches of Ulster and old Belfast* (Belfast, 1946).

Ó Ciosáin, Niall, 'The Poor Inquiry and Irish society' in *Transactions of the Royal Historical Society*, xx (2010), pp. 127–39.

O'Hanlon, William Murphy, *Walks among the poor of Belfast and suggestions for their improvement* (Belfast, 1853) (reprinted Wakefield, 1971).

O'Neill, Henry, 'The progress of sanitary science in Belfast' in *Journal of the Statistical and Social Inquiry Society of Ireland*, xi (1901).

O'Reilly, Des, *Rivers of Belfast: a history* (Newtownards, 2010).

Owen, D.J., *A short history of the port of Belfast* (Belfast, 1917).

Phoenix, Eamon, *Two acres of Irish history: a study through time of Friar's Bush and Belfast, 1570–1918* (Belfast, 2001).

Pilson, James Adair, *History of the rise and progress of Belfast, and annals of the County Antrim* (Belfast, 1846).

Radford, Mark, '"Closely akin to actual warfare": the Belfast riots of 1886 and the RIC' in *History Ireland*, vii, no. 4 (winter 1999), pp. 27–31.

Rodgers, Nini, *Equiano and anti-slavery in eighteenth-century Belfast* (Belfast, 2000).

Rodgers, W.R., *The return room* (Belfast, 2010) (broadcast by Northern Ireland Home Service, 23 December 1955).

Royle, Stephen A., *Belfast, part II, 1840 to 1900: Irish historic towns atlas no. 17* (Dublin, 2007).

—, 'The socio-spatial structure of Belfast in 1837: evidence from the First Valuation' in *Irish Geography*, xxiv, no. 1 (1991), pp. 1–9.

Scott, Robert, *A breath of fresh air: the story of Belfast's parks* (Belfast, 2000).

Sweetnam, Robin and Nimmons, Cecil, *Port of Belfast, 1785–1985: an historical review* (Belfast, 1985).

Thackeray, William Makepeace, *The Irish sketchbook* (London, 1842).

Thomson, James, *On public parks in connexion with large towns, with a suggestion for the formation of a park in Belfast* (Belfast, 1852).

Waller, Phillip J., *Town, city and nation: England 1850–1914* (Oxford, 1983).

Young, R.M., 'Old times in Belfast' in *Journal of the Royal Society of Antiquaries of Ireland*, xxxv, no. 4 (1905).

Manuscript sources

Annual report of the Linen Merchants' Association, 1873–1915 (PRONI, D2088/11/2).

Belfast 1837 valuation field books (PRONI, VAL/1/B/74A).

Belfast Corporation minutes, 1844–1896 (PRONI, LA/7/2/EA/1–21)

Book: problems of a growing city: Belfast, 1973 (PRONI, ENV/17/11/4A–B).

G.K. Smith and W. Hughes, Chronological statement in reference to the origin and operations of the Belfast Charitable Society (LHL, BPB1879/7).

John Black to George Black, 18 July 1765 (PRONI, D1401/5).

John F. Bateman, Report on the supply of water to the town of Belfast, 1855 (LHL, N3283).

Material regarding the history of tramways, 1877–1970 (PRONI, LA/7/26/M/1).

Memorial of the sawyers of Belfast, 22 May 1843 (BL, Peel papers, ccccxxxiii, Add MS 40613, f. 66b).

Miscellaneous notes for Benn's history of Belfast, *c.* 1870–7 (PRONI, D3113/4/7).

Notes re the history of Belfast, *c.* 1959 (PRONI, D1239/14).

Printed petition to the House of Lords and the House of Commons, 1813 (BL, Peel papers, l, Add MS 40230, f. 136).

Proclamation by the lord lieutenant, 11 March 1793 (BL, Peel papers, cl, Add MS 40330, f. 183).

Proposals of the proprietors of the Belfast Gas Works after the transfer of the contract from the Commissioners of Police to the company, 1826 (PRONI, Belfast Corporation Gas Works papers, D2177/1).

Reverend Anthony McIntyre, Diary kept by the Reverend Anthony McIntyre, 1853–6 (PRONI, D1558/2/3).

Rules and regulations for the House of Industry, Belfast, to be laid before a general meeting of the town for their approbation, 1810 (LHL, BPP32).

William Topping, Memoirs of the working life of William Topping, 1903–1956 (PRONI, D3134/1) (published as *A life in Linenopolis: the memoirs of William Topping, Belfast Damask weaver, 1903–1956* (Belfast, 1992)).

Wm Bald, FRS, Civil Engineer to [Board of Works, Dublin?], May 1834 (PRONI, Wallace papers, T1009/268, pp. 9–17).
Workman Clark Ltd, shipbuilders and engineers, 1880–1933 (PRONI, D2015/2/2).

Government publications

'And to be judicially noticed', H.C. debate, 6 July 1865, clxxx, c. 1184 (http://hansard.millbanksystems.com/commons/1865/jul/06/and-to-be-judicially-noticed#S3V0180P0_18650706_HOC_329) (25 August 2011).
'Belfast Corporation Bill (by Order)', H.C. debate, 6 March 1896, xxxviii, cc. 310–17 (http://hansard.millbanksystems.com/commons/1896/mar/06/belfast-corporation-bill-by-order) (25 August 2011).
Appendix to the first report of the commissioners appointed to inquire into the Municipal Corporations in Ireland [27], H.C. 1835, xxxvii, 199.
Belfast municipal boundaries: copy of Captain [Francis Y.] Gilbert's report upon the proposed extension of the boundaries of the borough of Belfast; together with copies of all documents laid before him, approving or objecting to such extension, H.C. 1852–3 (958), xciv, p. 2 and Appendix K (no. 6).
Belfast Riots Commission, *Report of the Belfast Riots Commissioners: presented to both houses of parliament by command of her majesty* (London, 1887).
Department of the Environment for Northern Ireland, *McMaster Street Conservation Area* (Belfast, 1994).
Report of the commissioners appointed to inquire into the state of municipal affairs of the borough of Belfast in Ireland [2470], H.C. & H.L. 1859, xii, 305.
Report of the commissioners of inquiry, 1864, respecting the magisterial and police jurisdiction, arrangements and establishment for the borough of Belfast [3466], H.C. 1865, xxviii, 27.
Third report of commissioners for inquiring into the condition of the poorer classes in Ireland [43] H.C. & H.L. 1836, xxx, p. 38.

Newspapers and periodicals
Belfast News Letter, 1739–1896.
Illustrated London News, 21 August 1886.
Irish Builder, 1890–98.
Irish Ecclesiastical Gazette, 21 June 1895.
Northern Whig, 15 July 1852.
The Times, 1793–1857.

INDEX